JACKSONVILLE

Riverport–Seaport

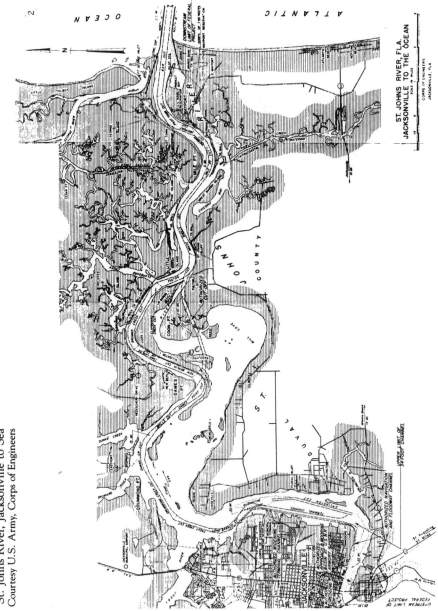

St. Johns River, Jacksonville to Sea
Courtesy U.S. Army, Corps of Engineers

JACKSONVILLE

Riverport—Seaport

GEORGE E. BUKER

University of South Carolina Press

STUDIES IN MARITIME HISTORY
William N. Still, Jr., Series Editor

Stoddert's War:
Naval Operations During the Quasi-War with France, 1798-1801
by Michael A. Palmer

The British Navy
and the American Revolution
by John A. Tilley

Iron Afloat:
The Story of the Confederate Ironclads
by William N. Still, Jr.

A Maritime History
of the United States:
The Role of America's Seas and Waterways
by K. Jack Bauer

Confederate Shipbuilding
by William N. Still, Jr.

Raid on America:
The Dutch Naval Campaign of 1672–1674
by Donald G. Shomette
and Robert D. Haslach

Lifeline of the Confederacy:
Blockade Running During the Civil War
by Stephen R. Wise

Admiral Harold R. Stark:
Architect of Victory, 1939–1945
by B. Mitchell Simpson, III

History and the Sea:
Essays on Maritime Strategies
by Clark G. Reynolds

Predators and Prizes:
American Privateering and Imperial Warfare, 1739–1748
by Carl E. Swanson

Honolulu:
Crossroads of the Pacific
by Edward D. Beechert

Wilmington:
Port of North Carolina
by Alan D. Watson

Jacksonville:
Riverport—Seaport
by George E. Buker

Copyright © 1992 University of South Carolina
Published in Columbia, South Carolina, by the
University of South Carolina Press

Manufactured in the United States of America

Library of Congress Cataloging-in-Publication Data

Buker, George E., 1923–
    Jacksonville, riverport—seaport / George E. Buker.
        p.   cm.—(Studies in maritime history)
    Includes bibliographical references and index.
    ISBN 0–87249–790–9 (hardcover : acid–free paper)
    1. Jacksonville (Fla.)—History, Naval. 2. Navigation—Florida—
Jacksonville—History. 3. Shipping—Florida—Jacksonville—
History. I. Title. II. Series.
F319.J1B89 1991
975.9'12—dc20   91-27169

Contents

Illustrations		vi
Acknowledgments		vii
Chapter 1.	French Rivals	1
Chapter 2.	The English Challenge	8
Chapter 3.	The False Dawn	15
Chapter 4.	One More Time	24
Chapter 5.	Frontier Engineers	32
Chapter 6.	Seminoles, Steamers, and a Seaport	39
Chapter 7.	The Blockade	51
Chapter 8.	The Inner Blockade	57
Chapter 9.	The Steamboat Era	73
Chapter 10.	Down to the Sea	88
Chapter 11.	Filibustering	99
Chapter 12.	Coastal Defense: St. Johns Bluff	117
Chapter 13.	Topographical Changes	128
Chapter 14.	Fire and Wars	136
Chapter 15.	The Container Revolution and the JPA	153
Notes		167
Bibliography		177
General Index		185
Index of Ship Names		190

Illustrations

St. Johns River, Jacksonville to Sea   frontispiece

following page 86

    Indian Tribes in Florida, 1562
    Inland Waterway, St. Marys to St. Johns
    James Grant's Mud Machine
    Union Gunboat at Mayport Mills
    Steamboats in Water Hyacinths
    Drawing of *Henry Burden*
    Air View of Mouth of the St. Johns River
    Blount Island with OPS Crane in Background
    Sketch of St. Johns Bluff Fortifications
    Three Friends Docking the USS *Constitution*
    St. Johns River, Jacksonville to Source
    U.S. Navy Instructors and Soviet Officers with
    Lend-Lease YPs at Mayport
    New Three Tier Loading at TMT

Acknowledgments

In 1974 I had the good fortune to receive a contract from the United States Army, Corps of Engineers, Jacksonville District, to write the district's history. This introduced me to the corps' importance in maritime development. Juan Colón, the chief of the district's public affairs office, encouraged me to continue my Corps of Engineers research by publishing several of my studies in the district's monthly paper, the *Drawbridge*. In 1989 I received a contract from the National Parks Service's Fort Caroline National Memorial to do a historical study of the Spanish-American War fortifications on St. Johns Bluff, Florida. This led me to a deeper investigation of a specific corps involvement in maritime affairs than that which I had pursued in my earlier work. These associations provided me with insights into port development which I might otherwise have overlooked.

I am grateful to the publications listed below for permission to reprint some of my previously published articles. I have revised these articles to some extent by the addition of recent research or tailored them to conform to the format of this work.

Chapter 3, "The False Dawn," was originally printed as "Governor Tonyn's Brown-water Navy: East Florida During the American Revolution, 1775–1778," in the *Florida Historical Quarterly*, vol. 58, 1979.

Chapter 8, "The Inner Blockade," was originally printed as "St. Augustine and the Union Blockade" in *El Escribano: the St. Augustine Journal of History,* vol. 23, 1986.

Part of chapter 9, "The Steamboat Era," was originally printed as "Engineers Vs Florida's Green Menace," in the *Florida Historical Quarterly,* vol. 60, 1982.

I wish to thank three individuals who assisted me, directly or indirectly, in forming the views I have expressed in this work. Edward A. Mueller has been a friend and source of information for a number of years. No one could write about steamboats in Florida without utilizing his research and writings. He is the authority in this field. The research done by two former students, years before I began work on this book, directed me to sources and concepts I might not have discovered on my own. Richard Apley Martin's term paper, "The River, The Road, and The Revolution," led to our joint publication of "Governor Tonyn's Brown-water Navy." The research of Robert M. Myers, Jr., on the Savannah sources of the inland waterway between the St. Marys and St. Johns Rivers gave me new insights into that project.

I owe thanks also to staff members of several libraries, especially to Hilda W. Federico and Anna K. Large of the Jacksonville University Library, Carol Harris of Jacksonville's Haydon Burns Public Library, and Elizabeth Alexander of the P. K. Yonge Library of Florida History.

I alone am responsible for any errors of fact.

JACKSONVILLE

Riverport–Seaport

Chapter One

FRENCH RIVALS

In the 1560s Jean Ribault brought his French Huguenots to the St. Johns River, and Pedro Menéndez de Avilés left Spain to drive him out. These actions transformed the St. Johns River from a potentially vast inland waterway, carrying settlers from a seaport at its mouth into the interior, to a military barrier between Spain and its French rivals to the north. The Spanish viewed the St. Johns as a huge moat protecting St. Augustine, and it retained that role for most of the next 260 years. In the early decades, the town and the river were vital to the defense of Spain's treasure fleets sailing home from its overseas empire.

Pedro Menéndez de Avilés, an able naval strategist, advised the Crown that a base should be built in Florida to keep the mainland shores clear of interlopers. This was crucial because the Spanish fleet, upon leaving Havana, sailed northward in the Gulf Stream until it reached the northern latitudes, wherein it could pick up the westerly winds for its journey back to Spain. The Crown accepted his plan, and, to insure its successful completion, appointed him *adelantado* (governor) of Florida in 1565 and governor of Cuba in 1567.[1]

By this time the French also had an interest in Florida. Earlier, Jean Ribault, commanding three ships sailing north off the coast of Florida, had come upon a place where the waters were boiling and tumbling over the shoals as if falling over rapids. Realizing this must by the mouth of a large river, he anchored for the night. The next day, 1 May 1562, he crossed the bar into the river, which he named riviere de Mai (River of May).

Ribault was not the first European to find this river. Some unknown Spaniard had observed the same phenomenon at the river's mouth and called it rio de Corrientes (River of Currents), a name found on many early maps dating from 1520. Later, after Pedro Menéndez de Avilés drove out the French, he established Fort San Mateo on the right bank at the river's mouth, and this name also was applied to the river. About 1590 the Spanish built the mission of San Juan del Puerto (St. John of the harbor) on an island at the mouth of the river, and from then until the British period in Florida, the river was known by both names, San Mateo and San Juan. The British anglicized San Juan to St. John's. When Florida became part of the United States, the apostrophe was dropped and the St. Johns River received its final name form. [2]

Ribault remained on the St. Johns for two days, trading with Chief Saturiba and his followers before resuming his search for a site to colonize. He continued northward until he reached a place he called Port Royal, where he left twenty-eight men to build Charles Fort while he returned to France for supplies. These men endured a series of misfortunes. After a fire burned their supplies and the Indians refused to give them more food, they built a small boat, and, with no navigator or compass, set out to recross the Atlantic. In mid-ocean they were becalmed and spent days watching their meager supplies dwindle. In desperation "they agreed that one should die to sustain the others [and] . . . his flesh was equally divided among his companions . . . "[3] Fortunately, they were picked up by a passing English ship before they had to make a second selection.

The governor of Cuba, hearing of this French settlement, dispatched soldiers to find and expel the intruders. They found the abandoned fort and a young French lad who had remained behind, preferring the known dangers of the Indians to the unknown dangers of an ocean crossing in a small boat. The Spanish destroyed the fort and took the lad with them to Havana.

Ribault, returning to a France torn by religious strife, fled to England where, at first, he was welcomed. The English even talked of using him to assist them in the New World. But later Ribault was placed in prison, where he languished for a year.

After the Peace of Amboise, in March 1563, Admiral Gaspard de Coligny, the leader of the Huguenots, returned to royal favor and continued his plan to create a Huguenot colony. In Ribault's absence, he selected René Goulaine de Laudonnière to lead three hundred men in three ships to the New World. On 25 June 1565, Laudonnière was back on the St. Johns River, building Fort Caroline about five miles from the river's mouth.

The artist Jacques Le Moyne, commissioned to record what he saw, was among the colonists. His *Narrative of Le Moyne surnamed De Morgues* included forty-two drawings and fifteen pages of description. After his death, his widow sold his pictures to Theodore de Bry who etched and published them in England in 1591. Le Moyne's originals were lost, but all of Europe became familiar with his work through de Bry's art.

Many of Laudonnière's colonists, when their expectations of immediate wealth were not fulfilled, looked elsewhere. Some of them stole two small boats to prey upon the Spanish ships passing up the Florida Channel (the Gulf Stream). One boat was captured, alerting the Spanish that the French were back. The other returned to Fort Caroline empty-handed. The discouraged Frenchmen began building a ship to return home.

It was at this time that the English trader John Hawkins sailed into the St. Johns to replenish his fresh water. Hawkins offered to take the Frenchmen back, but, fearing they might be held in England, they refused his offer. However, they traded for some guns and ammunition from the Englishman before he departed. Then they returned to their shipbuilding. Before they could leave, Jean Ribault arrived with five hundred soldiers in seven ships. Ribault took command from Laudonnière and immediately prepared for a Spanish attack he knew would come.[4]

Pedro Menéndez, learning of France's second attempt in Florida, assumed the task of driving them out. Commanding five ships, he briefly investigated Dolphin Bay south of the St. Johns River before hurrying on to meet the French. When he arrived, he found some of the smaller French ships inside the bar while the larger ones were anchored outside. As he prepared to attack, the ships outside the bar slipped their anchors and fled. Menéndez decided not to risk crossing the shallow bar with French forces in front of him and others at sea behind him. He sailed south to Dolphin Bay (which he renamed St. Augustine) where he crossed an equally shallow bar into the harbor and began off-loading and making preparations for his defense.

On 10 September Ribault, with 200 sailors and 400 soldiers, sailed south to find Menéndez. He left 240 men at Fort Caroline, half of them too ill to fight. Arriving at the St. Augustine bar, he found the water too low for him to bring his ships in. He decided to wait for higher water. Unfortunately for Ribault, a northeast storm arose and drove his ships south.

Menéndez took advantage of this storm to march overland to Fort Caroline, employing 16 axmen to clear the way. Four days later he fell upon the fort. In the ensuing action Menéndez's men killed 138 Frenchmen and captured 50 women and children and 6 noncombatants (drummers and trumpeters). The remaining 60 Frenchmen escaped into the wilderness. Two days later they fled in two ships to France. Among these survivors were Jacques Ribault, the son of Jean Ribault, Laudonnière, and Le Moyne. Menéndez left 300 soldiers at the captured fort, renaming it Fort San Mateo, while he returned to St. Augustine to plan his next move.

Later Menéndez learned from Indians that the French ships had been wrecked and that a group of Frenchmen were stranded south of an inlet below St. Augustine. He took 50 men to the inlet, where he parleyed with the Frenchmen. He ferried them over the river 10 at a time, gave them food and drink, and bound them in groups of 10. When all 208 were accounted for, he killed all but 10 professed Catholics.

On 10 October Ribault and the remainder of his men arrived at the inlet. Again Menéndez parleyed. Ribault and 150 men crossed over to the Spanish side. Menéndez spared only 16 (12 fifers, drummers, and trumpeters, and 4 Catholics). The inlet became Matanzas Inlet (the Place of Slaughter).

The 170 who had not trusted the Spaniard turned south, and at Cape Canaveral, where the *Trinity* had been beached, they turned to building defenses and a boat. On 26 November, Menéndez found them and promised that they would be sent back to Europe as prisoners. One hundred and fifty agreed, and Menéndez kept his promise. No one knows what happened to the remaining twenty.

Apologists for Menéndez point out that the French greatly outnumbered the Spanish, and they presented a serious security threat if brought back to St. Augustine as captives. They say that the final 150 were spared because their numbers no longer posed a threat.

Menéndez kept St. Augustine as his port of entry for Cuban and Spanish goods. Late in 1565 the supply ship *San Andrés*, a 65-ton, single-deck shallop, attempting to bring goods directly to Fort San Mateo, grounded crossing the bar, and the swells demolished her. This disaster influenced the Spanish to look for a safer route to supply their outposts on the St. Johns. Henceforth, goods were carried overland along the Indian trail running west from St. Augustine to the river, and then shipped downstream. Occasionally supplies were sent to San Mateo from St. Augustine, but the overland route proved more reliable.[5]

Two years later, in June 1567, Dominique de Gorgues sailed from France on a punitive expedition to avenge the killing of Ribault and his men. He made contact with Chief Saturiba, and the joint forces attacked and killed all the Spaniards at San Mateo.

This ended French colonization attempts in Florida until the following century, when they settled on the Gulf of Mexico.

However, this did not end French influence in the region. Many French pirates and privateers used the coast to establish camps from which they preyed upon the Spanish treasure fleet on its annual convoy to Spain, and woe to the poor sailors who fell behind the main fleet. These stragglers were fair game for the taking. In 1578 Governor Pedro Menéndez Marqués led a Spanish force up the east coast to drive out these French intruders. He captured about a hundred men and killed the leader, Nicolas Estrozi, a pirate who had sailed in the Caribbean. Estrozi had many friends among the Caribbean pirates, who retaliated by attacking Spanish forces in Florida during the next two years.

In 1586 Sir Francis Drake, returning home from a raid in the Caribbean, paused long enough to launch an attack upon St. Augustine. The town, now twenty years old, was inhabited by three hundred men, women, and children. The wooden fort was not well-built (construction of the Castillo de San Marcos was not begun until 1672), so the civilians fled inland to the Indian villages, leaving eighty men to defend St. Augustine. Drake landed a thousand men on Anastasia Island. Late in the day, as he crossed over to the mainland, the Spanish defenders fled. Drake burned everything and carried off a treasure chest of two thousand pounds sterling.

For the remainder of the sixteenth century there was growing discontent among some Spaniards over the site of St. Augustine. In 1600 the Crown held a hearing in Florida on these charges. Ultimately the defenders of the site prevailed. They said that, while it may not be the best place for colonization, it certainly was an excellent defensive post. The shallow bar at the harbor kept large ships out, yet the area inside for anchoring smaller ships was adequate. They also pointed out that there was no harbor closer to the Florida Channel, and if it was abandoned, some other nation would settle in that area to the detriment of Spain. Finally, the defenders noted the fact that the site was cut off from the interior by the St. Johns River moat, which was defensively sound.[6] The consensus was that Pedro Menéndez's selection was correct. For the remainder of the Spanish occupation of Florida, the presidio and the town of St. Augustine were the military and administrative headquarters of Spain's territory on the east coast of Florida. And during this period the St. Johns River was considered the last natural military barrier between Spain and its northern enemies.

Chapter Two

THE ENGLISH CHALLENGE

In May 1670, the English Lord Godolphin negotiated the Treaty of Madrid to bridge the gap between Spain's and England's concepts of colonization in the New World. Spain claimed that all of the land belonged to her by right of discovery, whereas England held that only actual occupation conferred exclusive rights of a nation to territory. In this treaty Spain recognized the existing English colonies in America. Neither party was aware that, during the month before this treaty was signed, 150 colonists from England and Barbados had landed 25 miles up the Ashley River to begin the settlement of Old Charles Town, South Carolina. Thus, from the Spanish view, Charles Town's colonists were interlopers, for at the time of the treaty the southernmost known English colony was on the Virginia border on the Albemarle Sound. The English, however, looked upon the treaty as agreeing with their position of effective occupation.[1] The Charles Town settlement led to English-Spanish rivalry in Florida until 1763, when England occupied all of Florida. It also brought warfare to the St. Johns, further delaying the development of a port and trade along the river.

The almost exclusive use of the Indian dugout on the St. Johns was another factor, most often overlooked, which impeded the growth of a port, or commercial trade, on the river. Seagoing vessels were hindered from crossing the bar by the shallow, treacherous channel at the river's mouth. However, the native-type craft served military needs on the river so completely that it further discouraged any attempt to develop the St. Johns valley for commercial oceangoing ships.

The Spanish developed an impressive dugout which they called a *periagua*, sometimes spelled *piragua* or *pirogue*. The periagua was the largest of the dugouts, generally built of two logs, but occasionally three logs were used. This vessel usually was powered by oars, but, if it operated upon open waters, it was fitted with the two-masted Bermuda sailing rig. Regardless of propulsion, the dugouts were suited to work the rivers and inshore waterways of the Southeast.[2]

Picolata, on the east bank of the St. Johns River, became the port for St. Augustine with respect to water travel on the St. Johns and for access to the inland waterways reaching north to St. Helena Island. Both the Spanish and the English used this water highway as a military route between their two colonies, which created further restrictions upon peaceful development of the St. Johns River.

Almost as soon as the English landed, Governor Francisco Guerra knew of the intrusion. Spanish Indians attacked an English landing party searching for food and water on Santa Catalina de Guale. The Englishmen were sent to St. Augustine as prisoners. Later Governor Guerra seized the English messengers sent to petition for the release of the prisoners. Guerra did this to cloak the military preparations being made to drive out the Englishmen.

Juan Menéndez Marqués commanded the three ships which sailed north in the Atlantic accompanied by fourteen periaguas of Indians moving up the inland waterway. Before Marqués attacked, a storm lashed the coast and his ships dragged anchors. To save his vessels, he withdrew to deep waters. Shortly thereafter, the English ship *Carolina* arrived with reinforcements. Marqués headed back to St. Augustine, and his Guale Indians drifted off. The first military confrontation settled nothing.

The two antagonists soon strengthened their positions. In 1672 the Spanish began the construction of the Castillo de San Marcos, a mighty coquina stone fort which defied later attacks by Spain's enemies. In 1680 the English, realizing the weakness of their position at Old Charles Town, moved their settlement to the confluence of the Ashley and Cooper rivers, where the New Charles Town was built. (In 1683 the name was changed to Charleston.)

In spite of the remoteness of these two colonies from the motherlands, much of the colonial competition along the Florida-Carolina border took place under the influence of the treaties and alliances drawn up in Europe. The decades of the 1680s and 1690s demonstrate the European link between the two colonies. In 1678 England was rocked by false disclosures of a Jesuit plot to assassinate the king and place his Catholic brother on the throne. News of this spread fear among the Englishmen in Charles Town who imagined that popish plots might be hatched in St. Augustine against their settlement. They organized their Indian allies and encouraged them to raid and harass Spanish Indians.

In 1682 the governor in St. Augustine acted. He organized an expedition to strike against the English Indians. But he was careful to limit his actions to the offending Indians. Peace between the mother countries in Europe kept both groups of colonists from attacking the other, but many messages passed between the two governors objecting to the actions of the other.

During the first four decades of the eighteenth century, military activity between St. Augustine and Charleston increased and the St. Johns River became more a military highway than the defensive moat of the previous century. Although there was peace in Europe between Spain and England, the English colonists continued to incite their Indian allies to make forays against the Spanish Indians, often as far south as the St. Johns River. In 1701, the governor in St. Augustine organized a punitive force to strike back. Eight hundred men, Spanish and Apalachee, marched north. Unfortunately for the governor, his Apalachee

Indians with their bows and arrows were no match for the gun-carrying Creeks. His punitive force was routed.

Meanwhile, Governor James Moore of South Carolina prepared a well-organized strike against St. Augustine. He had been informed by his contacts in England that war was about to break out in Europe between England and Spain, and he wanted to have the advantage of the first strike. His sources were correct, and the War of Spanish Succession, called Queen Anne's War in the colonies, began that summer. Moore made his move on 10 September, leading five hundred Carolinians and three hundred Indians south. Using fourteen small ships and periaguas, he sailed toward St. Augustine. Moore split his command. Colonel Robert Daniel in the periaguas paddled up the St. Johns River, landed where the Apalachee Trail crossed the river, and marched east to invest St. Augustine. Moore sailed directly to the St. Augustine harbor entrance.

The Spanish governor, forewarned of the attack, withdrew to the Castillo where he prepared for a long siege, and the coquina walls proved impervious to the small field pieces the Carolinians had brought with them. Both commanders sent messages for help before the actual siege began. Havana, the first to react, sent two men-of-war, a brigantine, and a sloop, to bottle up Governor Moore's small fleet. Three days later, Moore burned his ships and the town before retreating to his periaguas on the St. Johns.[3]

Moore's lack of success, the high cost of his expedition, and the paucity of booty or captured slaves made the governor quite unpopular in South Carolina. It was to restore his reputation that he organized, at his own expense, another expedition into Spanish territory. In January 1704, his fifty whites and a thousand Indians struck at Apalachee. This time he was successful. He captured 325 Indian braves and many more women and children, all of whom were brought back as slaves, which lifted the spirits and finances of many Carolinians.[4]

Later, in 1708, John Barnwell sailed up the St. Johns on another Indian slave-catching raid. The St. Johns River now became the usual route for such expeditions deep into the interior.

Under these blows from the English, the Spanish Indians were decimated, and the peninsula depopulated. There were no Spanish missions north of St. Augustine, and the Castillo was the only protection the colony had.[5]

In the War of the League of Hanover, when the two mother countries again were at war in Europe, Colonel John Palmer marched south to attack the Yamasee people living at Nombre de Dios, an Indian village in sight of, but beyond gun range of, the Castillo. The Spanish governor refrained from making a sortie from the safety of the Castillo. Four months later a Yamasee war party retaliated by capturing several Englishmen and sending them back to St. Augustine for safekeeping.[6]

In 1733, under the leadership of General James Oglethorpe, the English moved into Georgia. The following year the Spanish built two small forts on the St. Johns River where the Apalachee Trail crossed the waterway: Fort San Francisco de Pupa on the west bank and Fort Picolata on the east bank. These developments were in preparation for the next conflict between the two colonial powers.

The War of Jenkins's Ear, the first conflict between England and Spain to begin in the New World, broke out in 1739. Soon after hostilities had been declared, Oglethorpe had his Scot Highland Rangers and two hundred Indians up the St. Johns to attack both Fort Pupo and Picolata. It was a decisive victory for the English. Oglethorpe left Captain Hugh Mackay in charge of the two forts while he returned to Georgia to organize his major campaign against the Spanish.

Oglethorpe then gathered 1,620 men, 7 warships, and 40 periaguas at Frederica for the assault upon the Castillo. Using the inland waterway, his periaguas brought his soldiers and Indians to the south bank of the St. Johns River near the mouth. Marching south, he invested St. Augustine. By 13 June Oglethorpe's men and artillery were in place and the Castillo came under intense fire.

The Spanish governor endured twelve days of siege before he decided to go on the offensive. At midnight on 25 June, he sent out a force of three hundred to surprise the English encamped at Mosa under the command of Colonel Palmer, the man who had destroyed Nombre de Dios in 1728. The counterattack succeeded in catching Palmer and his men completely by surprise. After less than an hour, seventy-two Highlanders lay dead, along with fifteen infantrymen and thirty-five Indians. The Spanish loss was light. This victory at Mosa turned the tide against the English. The English command seemed to lose its ability to be decisive, and, with the arrival of seven ships from Cuba, the English siege was over.[7]

Two years later it was the Spaniards' turn. In the spring the governor gathered nineteen hundred men (including armed blacks) to invade the English settlement on St. Simons Island. Five men-of-war escorted the forty-nine small boats (periaguas, launches, galleys, and half-galleys) up the coast. On 16 July, the governor sent in fourteen ships to duel with the English artillery to gain access to the inland waterway. Although the Spanish lost a galley and two dugouts, they gained their objective, and the English at Fort Frederica prepared for the assault.

Unfortunately for the Spanish, the two patrols sent out to scout the land and prepare the way for the main body became lost in the marshes on the eastern edge of the island. Although the patrols found each other, they were still lost in the marsh. General Oglethorpe's scouts reported that the Spanish were wandering around in the marsh completely confused. Oglethorpe seized the opportunity to attack. The Battle of Bloody Marsh was as important a victory for the English as the previous attack upon Colonel Palmer had been for the Spanish.[8]

From 1743 to 1763 the border was quiet, but the governors continued to build their defenses in preparation for the next skirmish. However, the next war, the Seven Years War in Europe (the French and Indian War in the Colonies) was between the English and the French. The Spanish did not enter on the side of France until 1762, when France had already lost the war. In the diplomatic maneuvering at the Peace of Paris in 1763, Spain swapped Florida for Havana (which had been captured by the

English), and France lost all of its holdings on continental North America. At last there was only one colonial power on the Atlantic coast, from the pole to the Gulf of Mexico and westward to the Mississippi River. It seemed as if the military function of the St. Johns River was at an end.

Chapter Three

THE FALSE DAWN

The English had to start from scratch when they moved into Florida. Only a handful of the three thousand Spaniards elected to remain. The new governor set out to build a viable colony. However, it took years to bring in settlers and still more time to find a commercial crop for Florida. Indigo, an immediate success, had the quality to compete with the best in the world's market. But after three or four years the soil was exhausted and could no longer produce indigo. Just before the American Revolution, Florida's naval stores became an important export. Unfortunately for port development, the Revolution cast the St. Johns River into the same defensive military role it had played for the Spanish. After the war, the nascent commercial growth was snuffed out as the colony once again changed sovereigns. The glow of the English experience proved to be an economic false dawn along the banks of the St. Johns River.

Governor James Grant's initial concern was luring settlers to his new colony. Under his guidance the King's Road between Fort Barrington on the Altamaha River in Georgia and St. Augustine became an important overland link. It crossed the St. Johns at the Cow Ford, the site of present-day Jacksonville. The term *ford* is misleading, for the river runs deep and rapid there; however, the St. Johns is at its narrowest, and it proved to be the best place to swim cattle from shore to shore. A ferry based on the left bank carried people and goods to the south shore, landing near the old Spanish post of San Nicolás.

Denys Rolle developed a successful plantation near Palatka, where he produced thousands of gallons of orange juice for export. He also shipped turpentine from his huge pine tract, and raised cotton, sugar, and indigo for England. He claimed that his thousand head of cattle roamed the finest range in North America.[1]

In 1774 Patrick Tonyn succeeded Grant as governor of East Florida. By this time some impressive plantations dotted the banks of the St. Johns River. Two years later, in 1776, the first commercial shipments of naval stores began on the St. Johns. Twenty-six vessels entered the river to gather their cargoes from the plantation docks. Many of the landowners gave up their other crops to concentrate on the profitable naval stores. The growth of this commodity was phenomenal. In 1779 about twenty-five thousand barrels were exported. The next year around thirty-seven thousand barrels were produced, and by 1782 some fifty thousand barrels were available.[2] But without an established port, many Englishmen at home were not aware of the value of East Florida; therefore, at the Treaty of Paris in 1783, England returned this colony to Spain.

The failure of the English to build a port on the St. Johns may be traced in part to Governor Tonyn's preoccupation with the American Revolution, and to his concept that the St. Johns River was a military barrier protecting the province from the Georgians. There were three communication routes between the two: a sea voyage in the Atlantic, a boat trip down the inland coastal waterway, and the King's Road. The road was cut by the St. Marys and St. Johns rivers in the frontier zone between the two colonies. Thus, the easiest and most direct route was by water, and, for armed intervention, the inland waterways proved the most accessible. This fact caused Governor Tonyn to direct his energies toward creating naval defenses on the St. Johns River to protect his province from the Americans, and he diligently pursued the task of maintaining some armed ships to guard the colony.

When Martin Jollie sent word that the Georgians were planning an attack, Tonyn was in a quandary.[3] Where was his naval protection? Without ships he would not be able to scout the St. Marys and the St. Johns rivers, nor fend off the rebel supply vessels traveling south along the inland waterways supporting the invasion. East Florida's defenses were weakened by the absence of naval ships.

Fortunately, the *St. John* and the *Hinchenbrook* arrived, giving Tonyn his badly needed ships. He sent the *St. John* and planter Jeremy Wright's sloop with a fifty-man infantry detachment to the northern border. His sudden show of force caused the Americans to retreat, ending the invasion for the time being.[4]

In May 1776, Governor Tonyn heard that the Georgians were planning to interrupt British cattle drives and to stage guerrilla attacks on plantations along the north side of the St. Johns River. He advised the loyalist settlers to drive their cattle to the south side at the Cow Ford. He also ordered Lieutenant Grant to reconnoiter. While on patrol, Grant sighted and detained a small rebel sloop, and, during this endeavor, he was attacked by a force of two hundred Americans who almost succeeded in boarding the *St. John*. Grant rallied his sailors, who, after a heated engagement, beat off the Georgians.[5]

The inhabitants of south Georgia apprehensively eyed the troop buildup in East Florida. Now it was their turn to fear a British invasion. From their point of view, the schooner *St. John* would be the spearhead of any attack coming up the inland waterways. The Georgians decided to send out an expedition for the express purpose of capturing the *St. John*. They mustered 240 men to man a schooner, a flat, and an auxiliary vessel to eliminate the *St. John*.[6]

On 5 August, when the American naval force passed Jekyll Island heading south, John Martin sent a messenger overland to warn Lieutenant Grant, who was on the St. Marys cooperating with Captain Colin Graham's detachment of infantry. Grant decided to go out on the open water to avoid being bottled up.[7]

There was an indecisive skirmish between Lachlan McIntosh's raiding party and Captain Graham's men before both groups broke contact and headed for their respective bases. The incident ended without a clear-cut victory for either side. Later, Colonel Augustine Prevost defended his retreat from the St. Marys to the Cow Ford by claiming that he needed naval support.[8]

The increasing severity of the border incidents gave Governor Tonyn much concern. He was aware of the importance of naval power along his northern frontier; therefore, he exercised his Admiralty commission to issue a letter of marque to Captain John Mowbray of the sloop *Rebecca*. He placed the *St. John*, the *Rebecca*, and the sloop *Tuncastle* on patrol on the St. Johns River in September to discourage overland rebel raids. Toward the end of 1776 Tonyn believed his defensive efforts were deterring the rebels from invading East Florida. He confidently wrote that "by means of the Sloop Rebecca whom I commissioned and stationed on the St. Johns River, the inland passage from Georgia is secured . . . and this town . . . has its coast at last well defended."[9]

The naval defense of the East Florida province remained the major concern of Governor Tonyn throughout 1777. British naval vessels and merchant ships continued to come and go. Tonyn's waterborne defense devolved upon Captain John Mowbray and his sloop *Rebecca*, for the schooner *St. John* had been condemned as unfit for service and was left idle in St. Augustine's harbor.[10] Mowbray was kept busy patrolling and scouting the enemy's movements to the north.

Reports reached Tonyn that another major American invasion was underway. He extended Mowbray's contract for another four months, and enlarged his East Florida provincial navy by pressing into service the *Meredith*, a recent arrival from England, mounting ten guns, and the transport *Hawke*. Captain Mowbray, a former Royal Navy officer, was placed in overall command.[11]

Indeed, an American invasion by land and sea was underway. Colonel Samuel Elbert, the commander, intended to bypass the swamps south of Savannah by sailing to the St. Marys River before coming ashore. A smaller force of Georgia militia led by Colonel John Baker marched overland via the King's Road to rendezvous with Elbert at Sawpit Bluff, Florida. Arriving first, Baker's men undertook a scouting mission and forced the British to retreat to the Cow Ford.

On 14 May, Lieutenant Colonel Thomas Brown, leading the East Florida Rangers (a loyalist militia) and Indian allies, sailed from the Cow Ford downriver to Trout Creek in a private sloop of war to scout the Americans. He debarked on the north bank of the creek. There was a brief skirmish before Brown returned to the Cow Ford. When he learned that the British regulars were ready to cross the St. Johns to engage the Georgians, he volunteered to scout for the regulars again. Brown established contact with the invaders and held them long enough for the regulars to arrive and defeat the Americans in the battle at Thomas Creek, the southernmost battle of the American Revolution. Two days after the engagement, Elbert's force arrived at Sawpit Bluff and rescued eighteen of Baker's men. Learning of the fate of the land invasion, Elbert returned to his ships and sailed back to Georgia.[12]

While the events near Thomas Creek were occurring, a lesser-known but significant sea battle was underway off East Florida. Governor Tonyn intended to have Captain Mowbray, then on station up the St. Johns, lead the other provincial defense vessels into the St. Marys. Mowbray brought the *Rebecca* and the *Hawke* to the mouth of the St. Johns, where he anchored, just outside the bar. The *Meredith* and the other small vessels followed suit, though remaining slightly upriver. Suddenly, and unexpectedly, a strong wind whipped up the sea, forcing Mowbray and his escort to make for open water.

During the process of going to sea, the *Rebecca's* lookout spied a rebel brigantine, which Mowbray immediately prepared to engage. His ship only mounted ten carriage guns. Mowbray soon discovered his disadvantage against the more heavily armed American brig, but he pressed on, and, as the distance between the ships decreased, a running fight ensued. Both captains were aggressive. Finally, Mowbray gained the upper hand when his fire silenced the rebels for about eight minutes. Mowbray then maneuvered to board. During this time the Americans resumed fire, and, as Tonyn later related, "an unlucky shot carried away the Sloop Topmast and rent the mainsail, which gave the Brigantine the advantage in sailing and the opportunity of flight."[13]

The damaged American vessel's decks were crowded with men. As she heeled over in the wind to flee northward, the *Rebecca's* detachment of soldiers began to fire upon them. Captain Mowbray observed many dead rebels lying on deck as the brig pulled away. Mowbray suffered only one dead and nine wounded, but, due to his damaged condition, he returned to St. Augustine. Governor Tonyn was delighted to hear of the *Rebecca's* triumph. He gave much of the credit to Captain Mowbray, lauding "his zeal, activity, and unwearied industry, on all different parts of service."[14]

The tension between East Florida and her northern neighbor did not lessen, although the amount of activity declined through the end of 1777. Tonyn was so suspicious of this lull that he requested another detachment of infantry for the *Rebecca,* which was by then fully repaired and back guarding the inland water passage.[15]

The climax of American efforts to subdue East Florida occurred in 1778. Once again naval matters remained a high priority; the *Rebecca,* joined by the schooner *Hinchenbrook* and the ship *Galatea,* the latter two of the Royal Navy, formed a powerful defense triad protecting the waterways approaching the colony. By virtue of his Royal Navy rank, Captain Thomas Jordon of the *Galatea* assumed operational command of the east Florida vessels. On 6 April, he decided to intercept the invading American ships at Frederica, on St. Simons Island, Georgia.[16]

On 28 April, 1778, Governor Tonyn reported the loss of the *Hinchenbrook* and the *Rebecca* in an engagement at Raccoongut on Georgia's inland waterway. He questioned the circumstances, and he requested a formal investigation. In the end, he concluded that Mowbray was faultless and had been acting under orders. The governor further justified Mowbray's actions by saying that the captain had "attempted to destroy the vessel before he left her."[17]

The loss of the *Hinchenbrook* and the *Rebecca* was a severe blow to the East Florida forces. Captain Jordon had hoped to seize the offensive, but the debacle at Raccoongut changed all of that. The momentum had swung to the Americans, and Jordon would have to await their next move.

By the end of April 1778, East Florida was facing a critical situation regarding the lack of coastal and riverine defense. With haste, the governor was forced to purchase three vessels. Tonyn named one of these, an armed ship carrying fourteen guns, the *Germaine,* possibly hoping to flatter Secretary of State Lord Germaine into sanctioning the expenditure. The *Germaine* was suited for her task; she had a shallow enough draft to cross all the local harbor entrances. Finding a crew to man his vessels proved more difficult. Tonyn finally had to bargain with the crew and agree to split whatever profits were to be made with them. The *Germaine* and two other vessels, the brig *Dreadnought* and the galley *Thunderer,* were converted into warships. Tonyn vowed his further intention of procuring as many privateers as could be had to protect the province.

Tonyn also had three floating batteries built and armed them with twenty-four-pounders taken from the fort at St. Augustine. These batteries were strategically located: one on the inland passage, one at the foot of St. Johns Bluff, and the third at the Cow Ford.[18]

On 30 June, Governor Tonyn learned that "five Gallies, two flats, and two Pettuguas carrying Cannon," laden with a considerable supply of provisions, were in Cumberland Sound awaiting an opportunity to enter Nassau Inlet.[19] His East Florida defense vessels were ready to challenge the American ships. He sent the *Germaine,* probably under the command of John Mowbray, the

Dreadnought, and the *Thunderer* to patrol the St. Johns River. Twelve days later his flotilla was strengthened by the timely arrival of two Royal Navy vessels, the ship *Perseus* and the sloop *Otter*.[20]

Captain Keith Elphinstone of the *Perseus*, the senior naval officer, formulated plans to engage the rebels. However, before his operation could begin, the Americans learned of the increased naval power and fled. Led by the *Perseus* and the *Otter*, Governor Tonyn's navy made an effort to overtake them, but time and distance were on the side of the rebels.[21]

Tonyn was ecstatic over the turn of events. He confidently predicted that "the check given to the Rebels [by] the floating Batteries and naval Armament in St. John's River, the dispositions in posting his Majesty's Forces and the Difficulties thrown in their way have made the rebels from all present appearances relinquish their Design against this Province."[22]

Through the summer of 1778, ships from East Florida continued to patrol the coastal waters. Then for the remainder of the war East Florida forces were away from the province on overland strikes against American strongholds in the rebellious Southern colonies. After the capture of Savannah and the eventual British occupation of Charleston in May 1780, all military threat to East Florida had ended, and with it the Revolutionary War on the inland waters in and around British East Florida.

An example of what might have been may be seen in the rise of St. Johns Town. In the 1770s William Hester owned a two hundred-acre tract of land on the seventy-foot-high bluff on the south shore overlooking the mouth of the St. Johns River. (Hester's Bluff later became known at St. Johns Bluff.) In 1779 he sold his land to Thomas Williamson, who divided the property into city lots and laid out two streets. Three years later, with the influx of Georgian and South Carolinian loyalists, St. Johns Town grew to a settlement of three hundred houses with fifteen hundred inhabitants. Further, it became the shipping center for the St. Johns River at a time when fifty thousand barrels of naval stores were being exported. But, of course, time had run out for

Governor Tonyn to build a seaport on the St. Johns River, for he already had orders to transfer East Florida to the Spanish and to begin the evacuation of the loyalists unwilling to change allegiance. By 1785 St. Johns Town was deserted.[23] Economic darkness replaced the false dawn.

Chapter Four

ONE MORE TIME

Once again European settlers were uprooted as the English left and the Spaniards returned, and the historical patterns of the past were repeated one more time. Warfare and violence continued on the river, the defenders of St. Augustine still looked upon the St. Johns as a natural boundary for defense, and the dugout remained the utility watercraft for the region.

By now Florida was not essential to Spain's colonial organization. It was a matter of national pride for Spain to retake Florida, and the few Spaniards in Florida lived in the two small villages of St. Augustine and Pensacola. Spanish control over middle Florida was minimal, and the peninsula became the homeland of the Seminole Indians and a haven for runaway slaves from Georgia, Alabama, and the Carolinas.

Governor Tonyn remained in Florida until 13 November 1785, overseeing the departure of the English. Governor Vicente Manuel de Zéspedes hoped that some of the English would remain, shifting their allegiance to Spain, but he was anxious for those migrating to leave.

Some former loyalists, who resented being uprooted again, became a lawless group known as "the banditti." Daniel McGirt, one of the more infamous banditti, had been a South Carolina patriot until his commanding officer tried to confiscate his horse,

Gray Goose. McGirt fled south on Gray Goose to Florida where the British commissioned him to help organize the East Florida Rangers, a loyalist militia. During the American Revolution McGirt and his men stole slaves and rustled cattle from the American rebels. Their actions were cloaked in the legality of harassing the enemy. They continued these endeavors after the war when the confused situation in East Florida aided such lawlessness.

Another class in Florida was the fugitive slave. Many had acquired great skill in handling the plantations' dugouts. Most of the fugitives from American plantations used the inland passage to reach Florida, although there were instances when the larger dugouts made an outside voyage. For instance, in September 1788, the slave Thomas brought twenty-one fellow fugitives safely through the roaring white water over the St. Johns Bar in a large canoe.[1]

When Juan Nepomuceno de Quesada became governor in 1790, he was uncomfortable with the colony's defense. He relied upon Colonel Carlos Howard, who spoke Spanish, English, and an Indian language, but he needed more than a colonel to watch over his riverine frontier. Thus the time was propitious for the arrival in Florida of John McQueen, a Georgian debtor fleeing from his financial obligations. John McQueen, of Philadelphia, married into a wealthy South Carolina family, then settled in Georgia. During the American Revolution he became a captain in the navy. He worked for George Washington on several diplomatic missions to France, where he associated with Thomas Jefferson, Marquis de Lafayette, and the Count d'Estaing. Almost immediately the governor appointed McQueen a captain in the Rural Militia.[2]

One of McQueen's first military actions as a Spanish officer was to lead some soldiers and sailors down the east coast of Florida to capture William Augustus Bowles, the Maryland loyalist who had become a leader among his Indian wife's people. He had declared the Indian State of Muscogee, and it was rumored that he had landed at Indian River, planning to attack a trading post on the upper St. Johns. McQueen was not successful in finding Bowles, but he did encounter and drive off several Bahamian boats engaged in wrecking on the Florida coast. For his efforts, the governor granted him Fort George Island at the mouth of the St. Johns.[3]

Yet John McQueen was most helpful to Governor Quesada not for his naval ability, but for his becoming a loyal Spanish citizen, and one who helped other American settlers in Florida to see the advantages of loyalty to the Spanish crown. For this role the governor granted McQueen a large tract of land just up-river from the Cow Ford, which McQueen called San Juan de Nepomuceno. In short order McQueen converted to Catholicism and became comfortable under his new allegiance as Don Juan McQueen.

Early in 1794 agents from the French Republic appeared in Georgia, recruiting men to invade East Florida, wrest it from Spain, and turn it over to the Republic. This event caused the governors of Georgia and Florida to set aside their differences to work together against the French. Georgia's Governor George Mathews was afraid that the United States and Florida might be swept up in the maelstrom of the French Revolution.

Governor Quesada, fearing that he could not defend the lands between the St. Marys and the St. Johns, issued a decree in January 1794 ordering the settlers to move south to the St. Johns. Don Juan McQueen instructed his overseer at his plantation near the Cow Ford to build shelters at the Cow Ford for the troops destined to defend the St. Johns.

Although French warships sailed into the St. Marys River in May 1794, they did not participate in any landings in Florida. General Elijah Clarke, an American, commanded the "French" forces on land. In the summer of 1795 the "French" marched upon Fort San Nicolás on the south bank of the St. Johns. Shortly after this, Colonel Howard counterattacked by sailing up the St. Johns with three ships: Howard commanded the *Santo Tomás*, a British brig of twenty guns purchased from a privateer for this effort; McQueen commanded the *Santa Mónica*, a ten-gun

Spanish schooner; and the *San Augustín del Patrón,* a galley, carried the remainder of the militiamen, Indians, and blacks. Hardly had the first two vessels' guns fired upon the fort before the rebels rushed to their canoes and fled up the winding creeks emptying into the St. Johns from the north bank. The "French" then retreated to Georgia.

In August, Howard, in command of the *Santo Tomás,* and McQueen, now commanding the gunboat *Titiritera,* crossed the St. Marys bar to drive the "French" from Amelia Island, which they did. About the same time, a detachment of Georgia militia from Coleraine attacked the "French" and drove them back to the Spanish side of the St. Marys. Spanish soldiers moved against the deteriorating "French" forces until the invaders dispersed and returned again to the civilian society whence they had come.[4]

When Governor Quesada left his post in East Florida in November 1795, one of his last acts was to appoint Don Juan McQueen Commander of the River Banks of the St. Marys and the St. Johns, in recognition of his naval service on both rivers.

In 1803 the land-rich and money-poor Don Juan McQueen sold his land grants of Fort George Island and San Juan de Nepomuceno to another, richer, former American, John Houstoun McIntosh. This McIntosh was a cousin of the more famous General John McIntosh who served during the American Revolution. John H. McIntosh had inherited Spanish lands south of the St. Marys from his father George McIntosh, but he also had holdings in Georgia. He did become a Spanish citizen, although his loyalty to Spain was dubious, as his later actions would demonstrate. John H. McIntosh named the former McQueen's lands, just upriver from the Cow Ford, Ortega.

That same year Zephaniah Kingsley arrived in Florida. Born in Scotland, his father moved the family to Charleston, South Carolina, when he was eight. The senior Zephaniah Kingsley, a loyalist, was banished from the colony in 1782 and his estate confiscated. Little is known of young Kingsley's life until he appeared in Florida. However, he had engaged in the slave trade, had connections in Africa, Brazil, and the West Indies, and had married an African, Anna Madgigene Jai. Near the end of his life he was interviewed in New York by the abolitionist writer L. Maria Child. When she asked where he had met his wife, he said: "On the coast of Africa, ma'am. She was a fine, tall figure, black as jet, but very handsome. She was very capable, and could carry on all the affairs of the plantation in my absence, as well as I could myself. She was affectionate and faithful, and I could trust her."[5]

Kingsley's physical appearance was as unique as was his life-style. To compensate for his small stature he always appeared in public on an especially tall white horse. He generally wore a Mexican poncho, a broad-brimmed hat on his head, and square-toed shoes with large silver buckles on his feet. Thus attired, he rode around his holdings supervising the myriad details which go into running a successful plantation.[6]

He was an astute businessman. He brought new crops to Florida and improved the native crops. On his first plantation, at Laurel Grove, just south of present-day Orange Park, he developed flourishing citrus groves and planted sea island cotton. He also harvested naval stores from the forest. He had this work performed by his newly arrived slaves as a seasoning process before he sold them. The result was that Kingsley's slaves always received the top price on the slave market, as much as fifty percent more than the price of an ordinary worker. In one year his endeavors earned him ten thousand dollars, an almost unheard-of sum for East Florida.[7] When Congress passed the Embargo Act of 1807, and declared the importation of slaves into the United States to be illegal, it brought great prosperity to Florida. Both Kingsley and McIntosh benefited as Florida's economy grew.

Many Americans looked to annex Spanish Florida, both East and West. Former Georgia Governor George Mathews, who considered Florida ripe for conquest, became an agent of President James Madison to carry out the secret plan of Congress to acquire Florida east of the Perdido River.[8]

Mathews's plan was simple. He gathered a group of land-hungry Georgians willing to invade Florida. Then he looked for an ex-American Spanish citizen to lead the revolt against the Crown. He selected John H. McIntosh, who readily accepted. Mathews counted upon President Madison to provide arms, supplies, and both army and navy assistance to his men, who called themselves the Patriots of East Florida. As soon as the king's officials were ousted, Florida would be offered to the United States. What Mathews did not expect was the vacillation of President Madison when the actual revolt took place.

On 12 March 1812, the Patriots crossed into Florida. But instructions from Washington for the American commanders were confusing and contradictory. Yet under the urging of Governor Mathews both the military and naval commands followed his Patriots into East Florida. Colonel Thomas Adam Smith moved his soldiers to the outskirts of St. Augustine. Commodore Hugh Campbell sent three gunboats to the St. Johns. One was stationed near the mouth of the river; the other two were off Picolata. Campbell ordered gunboats 62 and 63 to St. Augustine with orders "not to offend the town or garrison unless in retaliation for an insult to the American flag."[9]

The Patriots invited the people to join them. Kingsley was asked but refused, suggesting he be considered a prisoner. He changed his mind when he found out that the Patriots were not taking prisoners; it was join the Patriots or be banished and lose all property.[10]

But all was not going well for the Patriots. On 18 June 1812 the United States officially declared war on Britain, and on 2 July the Senate rejected a bill authorizing the President to occupy the Floridas.

On 10 July, at Fernandina, the Patriots held a constitutional convention which elected John Houstoun McIntosh as the convention president. Two weeks later, at Kingsley's Laurel Grove plantation, McIntosh became the Director of the Territory of East Florida. Thus there was political action even though the military positions were at a standstill.

However, Sebastián Kindelan, the new Spanish governor, played upon the Indians' apprehensions. His agents told the

Seminoles that if Spain was conquered they would stand alone against the Americans.[11] The Alachua and Alligator tribes, joined by some of the braves from several of the upper Creek towns, as well as forty blacks, responded to Kindelan's call for arms. Almost 250 warriors swept down upon the St. Johns, striking at the scattered plantations. Then swiftly they moved toward the American camp outside of St. Augustine. The Seminoles killed eight or nine soldiers and freed eighty or ninety slaves. The Patriots shouldered their arms and fled, leaving Colonel Smith to face the Indians and the Spanish. The Americans retreated back to the St. Johns to the protection of the navy's gunboats. On 9 August 1812, Governor Kindelan announced that the investment of St. Augustine had ended, and his black militia had made contact with the Seminoles, who were driving cattle into St. Augustine to relieve the town's food shortage.[12]

The fortunes of Zephaniah Kingsley and John H. McIntosh moved in opposite directions as a result of the Patriots War. McIntosh lost considerable money and property, whereas Kingsley continued to make money by importing slaves. In 1813 Kingsley bought Fort George Island from McIntosh. Kingsley built a fine two-story house, which still stands on the island, and established his wife and household at the mouth of the St. Johns, where he could watch over his slave operations. After his death, his executor collected $77,322 from the United States government for the property damages he had incurred because of the Patriots War. Payment was made under article 9 of the treaty transferring Florida from Spain to the United States.[13]

An example of Kingsley's business acumen, and the complacency with which some American officers charged with preventing the slave trade operated, may be illustrated by the captain of a revenue cutter who had captured a slaver with 350 slaves on board. It was one of Kingsley's ships. Yet the captain turned over the rescued slaves to Kingsley because he was the only man available with the means of caring for so large a number of slaves![14]

Americans living contiguous to Spanish Florida were disturbed by the lawless conditions along the frontier region separating the two countries. Cattle rustling was a way of life on both sides of the border. American slaveowners were convinced the Seminoles were encouraging and even carrying off slaves to the safety of their villages under the Spanish flag. The runaway slaves owned cattle and lived a relatively free existence away from white men's control, which was not the proper life to flaunt before the American plantation system. As a further affront, Spain stationed black troops in Florida, an example fraught with danger for the institution of slavery.[15]

Under these conditions, the situation deteriorated to the point where President Monroe sent General Andrew Jackson with an army into Spanish Florida to punish the Seminoles. The action became known as the First Seminole War, 1817–1818. General Jackson exceeded his orders, calling upon him to respect all posts flying the Bourbon flag. Indian villages were burned; the Spanish settlements of Pensacola and St. Marks were occupied; and two British subjects were captured, tried, and executed. The South was jubilant, Spain and Britain outraged, and the Seminoles impressed.

President Monroe promptly returned Jackson's conquest to Spain, but the Spanish Crown knew its ability to restrain the dynamic, aggressive Americans was weak enough to encourage the Americans to embark upon outright conquest. In order to salvage as much as possible, Spain entered into diplomatic talks with the United States. The following year the Adams-Onís Treaty ceded Florida to the United States, although the formal transfer did not take place until July 1821. Thus was the territory of Florida obtained by the Americans, and the St. Johns River ceased to be a military boundary protecting St. Augustine.

Chapter Five

FRONTIER ENGINEERS

The transfer of Florida to the United States placed upon the nation the same tasks that it had had when it received the Louisiana Territory from France in 1803. Then, President Thomas Jefferson immediately had sent out survey teams to study the land so that it might be protected, settled, and developed. Now these same tasks were necessary for Florida.

The interior of the peninsula was terra incognita in 1821 when William Simmons, an author writing about Florida, attempted to pierce its darkness. He gathered all the sources of information he could find to amplify and enlarge upon his own knowledge of the territory. Simmons concluded that south of the St. Johns River the peninsula consisted of a large basin which probably provided waters to the St. Johns as well as rivers in the southern part of Florida. He speculated that it would be an easy matter to connect the St. Johns with the Indian River on the east, with the Caloosahatchee, which flows into the Gulf of Mexico, on the west, and with Lake Mayaco in the center of the peninsula, thus opening inland navigation throughout the territory.[1]

Such reports of the impassability of land transportation coupled with the enticing prospects of extensive waterways caused the settlers of Florida to call upon the federal government for aid. Of course, the Territory of Florida was not the only part of the

United States to need the technical engineering services that only the U.S. Army Corps of Engineers could provide. (West Point was the first engineering school in the United States; Rensselaer Polytechnical School was not founded until 1824, and its first graduates were not sent forth until the 1830s.) The whole nation was bursting with projects to develop communications systems, open transportation routes (both roads and canals), and tame rivers—in a few words, to promote progress. The hue and cry from all parts of the country was for government participation in these sectional projects; the local resources were not enough to carry the cost nor supply the technical talent.

Congress reacted in April 1824 to the demand of its constituents by passing a Rivers and Harbors Act and a Canals and Roads Act which put the Corps of Engineers into the midst of the nation's expanding civil programs. Now that the way was clear for the civil projects so badly needed to develop Florida, there was a flurry of tasks performed by the corps to bring progress to the territory. One of the first, though unsuccessful, endeavors was the survey for a canal across the peninsula to link waterborne traffic from the Gulf of Mexico with that of the Atlantic coast, bypassing the lengthy, treacherous reefs and shoals of the Florida Keys. [2]

In March 1826, General Simon Bernard of the Board of Internal Improvements drew up plans for this survey. In the spring of 1827 Bernard visited Florida to personally examine the terrain over which the earlier survey party had worked. When he returned to Washington, he called upon President John Quincy Adams to state that he believed a ship canal across Florida was impracticable. The most that could be done would be to construct a canal six feet deep for steamboats, and the final result did not justify the expense and effort. He did recommend a canal from the St. Marys to the St. Johns as part of the contemplated inland waterway along the Atlantic coast. [3]

James Gadsden was one of the early engineers in Florida. Born in Charleston, South Carolina, he joined the army soon after he graduated from Yale in 1806. During the War of 1812, he served as a lieutenant in the Corps of Engineers. After the war he aided

Andrew Jackson in surveying the military defenses of the Old Southwest and the Gulf Coast, and he was with Jackson during the First Seminole War. His friendship with Jackson helped his military career so that in late 1820 he served as Adjutant General of the Army. When the Senate refused to ratify his appointment, he was miffed, resigned his commission, and moved to Florida to start life anew. Gadsden remained in the Territory for the next sixteen years, maintaining continual communication with the Chief of Engineers in Washington, proposing engineering undertakings, supervising assigned projects, and recommending competent individuals in Florida to act for the Corps.[4]

In 1828 James Gadsden was given supervision over the Florida project. He surveyed the area between the St. Marys and the St. Johns and felt that a canal could be cut and, with the deepening of several shoal spots, a passage could be made which would allow vessels of thirty or forty tons to pass through at low tide without difficulty. He advertised for laborers for this work, but only Zephaniah Kingsley submitted a bid for the task. Earlier, Kingsley had submitted a bid to improve the Talbot Dividings for $3,500 more than the total appropriation of $13,500 which Congress had set aside to connect the two rivers.

Gadsden talked Kingsley into a new contract by which Kingsley would complete the canal, line the mouth of the canal with a stockade of palmetto logs to prevent sand bars from forming, open the Talbot Narrows, and remove the oyster beds from the Sisters waterway. All of this was to be done for $13,500.

Before Kingsley could begin dredging operations he had to send his crews out to clear the channel of snags (a general term for any submerged artificial obstruction in a waterway). The majority of snags were trees and large branches which had fallen into the water. Snagboats, for removing these underwater barriers, usually consisted of two large flats, fifty or sixty feet long, joined together with an eight-foot space intervening. Over this space a windlass was mounted to raise the snag to the surface.

Gadsden found that the marsh was made up of a soft mud, almost in a liquid state. Therefore, it would be difficult to dig too deeply into the channel bottom without disturbing the banks. But he felt that, as the weight of the removed earth settled on the banks, it would firm the sides, allowing the channel to be dug to greater depths. Thus, he was willing to do some work, let it settle, then return to digging. In addition, he felt that during the winter months, when work had stopped, the currents, helped by the initial digging, would scour the channel deeper, saving him some expenses.[5]

Not all of Gadsden's problems were caused by nature. At one time, while Kingsley was absent from Florida, Gadsden issued some new instructions to Kingsley's agent, who was hesitant to carry them out. After considerable thought, the agent decided not to do anything without Kingsley's permission, for his employer was a strange man who defied convention. Therefore, the agent shut down all work.[6]

The following year Gadsden reported some success. The initial cleaning and digging had strengthened the current during the change of tides, and the expected scouring had taken place. However, the earth placed upon the banks had not strengthened the banks to allow noticeable deepening. In fact, the banks were as susceptible to sliding into the canal as before. He realized that he should have made the canal wider initially so that the sliding banks would not fill up the center channel.

In July 1830 Gadsden reported that navigation between the St. Marys and the St. Johns was open for coasting schooners drawing not more than five or six feet. But he stated that the schooners had to pass the Amelia Cut at the north, or the Sisters Cut at the south, at an early stage of the flood so as to reach the Talbot Dividings at a favorable stage of half or full tide. He knew that such timing would keep them from being impeded at the Talbot Dividings.[7]

By September 1832 Gadsden reported that dredging by shovel was not successful. The crews could only work during the warm months, and the liquid mud was difficult to shovel out of the channel. The shovel men were exposed to the elements out in the marsh, with no protection. Even worse, they could work only between the ebb and flood tides, which was a small portion of the day. But Gadsden had a solution. He requested that one of the new steam-powered mud machines be provided. He knew that one of these machines was working on the St. Marks river in Florida; if he had a mud machine he could protect his men from the elements, he could haul the dredged material farther away from the delicate channel banks in flat boats, and he could go deeper than his shovel men could dig.

Gadsden was talking about one of James Grant's mud machines. Grant, a mechanic of Baltimore, had built several machines for the Corps of Engineers. Basically, his device was an endless chain of buckets on a frame which could be attached to a flat or a boat so that the buckets could be lowered to the bottom, and, when the steam power was engaged, the buckets would revolve, bringing up the mud or sandy material from the river bed.[8]

Press of other business made it necessary for Gadsden to give up his supervision of the St. Marys-St. Johns excavation before he received an answer to his request for a mud machine. But, concerned that his departure would hinder Jacksonville's outlet to the sea, he recommended Lieutenant S. W. Harris, then stationed at Fort King in Florida, to replace him. He also suggested that Harris be sent to West Florida to work on the St. Marks mud machine to gain experience while he waited for one to be assigned to Jacksonville.

The Chief of Engineers did not act upon Gadsden's request. He felt that the cost of a mud machine exceeded the appropriations allocated for the waterway. The Chief decided that the mud machine at work at St. Marks, or the one working on the mouth of the Savannah River, should be sent to the waterway when available. Meanwhile, he shut down the work on the St. Marys-St. Johns channel.[9]

It was March 1835 before the Corps of Engineers ordered a renewal of the inland navigation project. This time Lieutenant Joseph K. F. Mansfield was assigned to supervise the work. First he ordered carpenters to repair the Savannah mud machine, and then to build mud-flats to haul away the dredged material. He planned to use the Savannah-built government steamer *Essayons* (named after the Corps of Engineers motto), to haul his mud-flats and dredge to the coastal workings. Mansfield hoped to commence operations on the inland waterway by January 1836. However, military operations of the Second Seminole War, which began in December 1835, disrupted his plans.[10]

In May 1836, Major General Winfield Scott, military commander in Florida, ordered that the *Essayons* be assigned to him for military operations. Scott ascended the St. Johns as far as Lake Monroe. The *Essayons* was the first steamer to steam on this lake. When Scott tried to continue south he found that the bar at the inlet to the lake was too shallow for the *Essayons*. General Scott referred to his commandeered ship as "a miserable little steamer."[11]

Finally Mansfield was able to assemble all of his watercraft for dredging. In July, in order to save both time and money, he requested permission to cut wood for the dredge from government land on Amelia Island. At the end of July he had to lay up his dredge because it was the sickly season when he could not hire hands to work in the marshes during the heat of summer. With the advent of cooler weather in the fall he was back at work on the narrows. Mansfield reported that his expenses were $1,950 per quarter ($650 per month). He broke down his monthly expenses as follows:

1 Captain Dredge Boat	$ 75.
1 Engineer	55.
mate & mudflats	45.
9 hands	210.
supplies	24.
1 man & 4 hands survey	241.
	$650.

In February 1837 the new military commander in Florida, General Thomas S. Jesup, needed his dredge boat to dredge the bar at

Lake George. Mansfield had to wait until the end of March for his dredge.[12]

In spite of all the military interruptions, Mansfield kept at it, and, at the end of 1837, he was able to report that he had cut a channel at the oyster banks between the Sisters, near the St. Johns River. He dredged a cut 3,680 feet long, 70 feet broad, and 3 feet deep at low water. He estimated about 2,990 cubic yards dredged. He still had to dredge 500 yards at the Amelia Dividings, and 1,400 yards at the Talbot Dividings. He acknowledged that it was slow going, but noted that the dredge could be employed only when it was afloat.[13] Thus he was at the mercy of the tides.

By 1839 the project was completed. The inland waterway between the St. Johns River and Cumberland Sound was in operation, the first step in opening Jacksonville and the river to the oceans of the world. These frontier engineers performed amazing feats using man or animal power and primitive steam engines. They too were frontiersmen who should be acknowledged along with the cattlemen and the plantation owners for developing the Florida Territory.

Chapter Six

SEMINOLES, STEAMERS, AND A SEAPORT

When warfare had come to the St. Johns River in the past, it had meant delaying any plans to build a port. But the Second Seminole War, 1835–1842, had the opposite effect. The Indian conflict provided a boost to port development, for the army employed steamers to support its logistics system in the roadless frontier territory of Florida. The St. Johns River, with its tributaries, offered ready access to the interior of the peninsula. The army used steamers to explore, transport troops, and supply its forts along these waterways, and, with few exceptions, these incoming and outgoing steamers stopped off at Jacksonville.

In the first year after Florida was transferred to the United States, the settlers around the Cow Ford laid out the initial streets for the creation of Jacksonville, in honor of General Andrew Jackson, Florida's first governor. That same month, June 1822, sixty-one citizens petitioned Secretary of State John Quincy Adams to designate their new municipality a port of entry, while pointing out the disadvantages of St. Johns Bluff.[1] Adams did not act on their petition. But a decade later, after Congress created the District of St. Johns, President Andrew Jackson selected Jacksonville as its port of entry.

Sailing ships frequently ascended the St. Johns as far as Lake George, although they often had to rely on row boats to tow them against wind or current on the river. But it took some time before a steamboat captain ventured into the St. Johns River from the active ports on the Atlantic coast. On 4 May 1829, the *Marine News* of Savannah noted that Captain Curry left port in the *George Washington* for the St. Johns River. At the end of the month it reported the arrival of Captain Curry from Jacksonville. It is not clear if these two entries report one or two voyages. The paper made no mention of any other steamboats plying between Savannah and Jacksonville in either 1829 or 1830. But the *George Washington* made other trips to the St. Johns in April and May 1831, and in May and June 1832. On 19 November 1833, the *Washington* arrived in Savannah from Picolata with a cargo of oranges and towing the steamer *Darien.*[2]

Captain Charles Willey's letters to his ship's owners in Maine illustrate schooner traffic on the St. Johns River. On 11 October 1831, Willey reported a seventeen-day passage from New York to the St. Johns. He had planned to go to Charleston, but the wind at the bar shifted, so he continued on another day to the St. Johns, where he crossed the bar without a pilot and without grounding. He passed a ship heading for New York with 135,000 oranges, but until he got upriver he could not tell what his freight would be.

On 29 October Captain Willey detailed his activities. He had traveled to the head of Black Creek, selling the following portion of his cargo:

Item	Price
Flour	$ 7.00
Mackerel	3.50 per half barrel
New Rum & Gin	.50
Potatoes	2.00 per barrel
Onions	2.75 per barrel
Pork	17.00
Salt (30 bags)	2.31½
Lumber	25.00

He noted that the New Brunswick Cider had leaked badly, and that the dry goods were dull sellers. He also said that he had deposited all the goods not sold with Calvin Roads of Mandarin, in case he should be lost at sea on his next voyage.

Captain Willey loaded 85,000 oranges as freight from the Fatio Plantation, for which he charged $3.50 per thousand. He then bought 80,000 oranges and 5,700 lemons for the ship's account. In addition, he took aboard four passengers at $16.00. (His letter gave no indication if that was per passenger or a total fee.) He directed the owners to write to him care of a dockside address in New York.

It took him twelve days to reach New York, where he sold 35,000 oranges at $18 per thousand. He sent 5,100 oranges and 550 lemons to the owners. Willey also picked up freight for a return trip to the St. Johns, and he said he would have to sell the remainder of his cargo, whatever the price. He calculated that he had made $525 on the oranges and cleared about $875 total for the voyage.

His return trip to the St. Johns took only six days. Willey waited a day and a night for a pilot, but weather prevented the pilot boat from leaving shore. The wind drove him onto the south breakers, and he was forced to jettison some of his deck load. Willey estimated his loss at $35. Worse yet, his schooner was damaged, forcing him to go to Charleston for repairs.[3]

Lieutenant William P. Piercy, U.S. Navy, commanding the one-gun schooner *Spark*, sailed up the St. Johns to check on live oak operations in 1831. His brief sojourn on the river demonstrates again the ineffectiveness of sailing ships. On 22 August, Piercy hove too off the bar waiting for a pilot. An hour later, the pilot brought him over the bar. Lt. Piercy anchored in four fathoms of water next to an American schooner. The next day, before 6:00 A.M., Piercy boarded the schooner to examine its cargo of live oak bound for the Navy Yard at Charlestown, Massachusetts. When the pilot came aboard, Piercy weighed anchor and made sail upriver. It took him until 1:00 P.M. the next day to beat against the wind and current to reach Jacksonville. He spent the rest of the day watering his ship.

At daylight on 25 August the wind had shifted 180°, so that when Piercy weighed anchor to exit the river he again had to beat against the wind. He anchored at midday and sent a boat ashore to get wood. Twenty-four hours later, Piercy resumed working downriver. Within two hours, he grounded on the south shore. Three hours later, when the tide changed, he hauled off to his kedge anchor and made sail for St. Johns Bluff. The next day he tried to beat downriver, but when the flood tide set in, at about half past eight, he had to anchor to keep from being carried upriver. With the changing tide, he finally was able to reach the mouth of the river and anchor near the schooner *Argo*, which also was waiting to leave the St. Johns.

At daybreak Lt. Piercy weighed anchor and stood down to the bar, but found he could not cross. The wind was off his head and there were heavy swells over the bar. He wore around to return to his former anchorage. A week later he got underway to stand down to the bar. This time it was light winds and a heavy swell which kept him from exiting. Again he wore around and returned to his anchorage. Finally, on 5 September, Piercy was able to stand out of the river, and "at 10 crossed the bar in $1\frac{1}{2}$ faths. water, hove too and discharged the Pilot. At 10.15 filled away & stood to the South^{d}."[4] Clearly steamers were less at the mercy of the elements than sailing ships.

In early 1834, the *Florida*, a 144-ton, side-paddle wheeler, built in Savannah specifically for the Savannah–St. Johns run, began once-a-week operations. She steamed from Savannah to Jacksonville and Picolata, the port for St. Augustine. Her advertisement listed her stops and stated that all slave passengers must be cleared through the Savannah Customs House before one o'clock. The *Florida* continued this schedule through December 1835, when the Second Seminole War broke out. In fact, on 23 December 1835, just three days before hostilities, she carried five army officers, who were en route to Fort King in the center of the peninsula, up Black Creek.[5]

The army employed steamers in combat operations during the Second Seminole War, the nation's longest and most costly Indian war. During this conflict the army brought a great number of steamers to the St. Johns, where they were used extensively for combat operations, and the steamers proved their worth. In the early years of the war, while the troops campaigned in the northern portion of the Florida Territory, the army used the St. Johns as its major waterway to reach the Indians. The Quartermaster Corps built its supply depot, Fort Heilman, at Garey's Ferry, on Black Creek near present-day Middleburg. But as time passed, the army built a series of forts stretching south along the river some hundred miles beyond Lake Monroe. Occasionally a shallow draft vessel might steam as far south as Fort Lane on Lake Harney, but beyond Fort Lane the army had to rely on poled or rowed canoes and dugouts.

The army immediately employed steamers. On 11 January 1836, the *Florida* steamed downriver carrying General Duncan Clinch to the St. Marys, where he hoped to enlist Georgians to volunteer for defense of the St. Johns settlers. The *Florida* passed the *Davenport* from New York carrying fifty soldiers headed for Fort King. Later, on 29 January, the *Florida* steamed into Jacksonville with the Richmond Blues from Virginia on their way to Picolata. The *John David Mongin* arrived in Jacksonville the same day with 116 volunteers from Savannah.[6]

The steamboat gave the military commanders in the field rapid communication with Washington. Fort Mellon in the interior was only five days from the nation's capital. A letter could leave Washington on Friday and arrive at Charleston the next Monday. Here it would be transferred to a small river steamer to be taken to Fort Mellon. The round trip from Charleston up the St. Johns took from Monday to Friday, and the Charleston packet departing Friday would arrive in Washington the following Monday.[7]

The army chartered most of the steamers it employed. The government had few steamboats of its own, and, believing that the war would be over soon, the Quartermaster felt that chartering the necessary vessels would be more economical than building a fleet just to fight Indians in Florida. The Quartermaster erred in his basic assumption about the length of the Indian conflict.

Of course, the military commanders were not adverse to using government vessels, when available. Time and again, Lieutenant Mansfield, working on the dredging project to open up the intracoastal canal between the St. Marys and the St. Johns rivers, had his government steamer ordered off the job to perform some military task in Florida. From 24 to 29 April 1836, General Winfield Scott used the *Essayons* to go up the St. Johns on a reconnaissance mission. Before the steamer was returned to Lt. Mansfield, Scott sent the *Santee* and the *Essayons* to Volusia to evacuate troops who had come down with yellow fever.

In July the *Essayons*, under the command of Captain Fenn Peck, transported troops up Black Creek to Fort Heilman. While steaming back to his dredging work, Peck found Colonel Hallowes on shore wounded, trying to attract attention. Captain Peck picked up Hallowes, along with several of his slaves, all refugees from a Seminole attack upon Hallowes's plantation. Peck carried them to Picolata. Two weeks later Peck steamed up Black Creek to Fort Heilman. En route he spotted and fired at some Indians on shore. Shortly after this trip, Captain Peck steamed to Picolata, where he towed Lieutenant Herbert's fifteen men and forty horses across the St. Johns in flats. The next night, on Black Creek, Peck sent his men out to gather wood for his steamer. At daylight he steamed down the creek to the St. Johns. Just as he appeared at the mouth of Black Creek, Lt. Herbert burst into view, followed by a band of Seminole warriors. Peck's yawl could carry only nine men at a time. His men covered Herbert's boarding by laying down heavy fire upon the Indians. During this skirmish the steamer was struck by many bullets, but no harm came to the crew.[8]

The *Essayons* was not the only equipment Lt. Mansfield lost to the war in Florida. In 1837, when General Thomas S. Jesup became the military commander, he repeatedly asked for Mansfield's dredge so that he could remove the bars on the St. Johns at lakes George and Monroe. Jesup wanted to make the St. Johns "an avenue for the transportation of troops and supplies near two hundred miles." Evidently the general was successful, for in November 1837, the *Santee* passed the *Camden* at the bar on Lake George guarding a dredge boat working to deepen the channel.[9] It is small wonder that Lt. Mansfield took so long to improve the waterway between the St. Johns and the St. Marys.

Gradually the army drove the Indians southward, and the theater of war shifted to the Everglades. The army decreased the number of chartered vessels on the St. Johns. But many steamers continued to operate out of Jacksonville, catering to the civilian demands developed during the war.

Early in 1841 Jacksonville's position as the port of entry was challenged by the citizens of Hazard, Florida. The town, later known as Mayport Mills before becoming Mayport, felt that the Indian conflict had created an erroneous assumption of the importance of Jacksonville. The citizens of Hazard desired to have the customs house moved to their community so that incoming vessels could file their papers immediately before going on to their ultimate destination. When the first petition was denied, the people of Hazard submitted a second and a third petition.[10] But nothing came of these requests to Congress.

In 1844 Master Edward Clifford Anderson, USN, boarded the *General Taylor* in Savannah just as she was leaving for Florida to check on the Indians and to prevent illegal lumbering of live oak timber. He commented on how dull the inland trip was, with nothing to be seen but an occasional clump of trees or a lonely plantation now and again. When a storm broke and heavy rain fell, Anderson brought a pitcher on deck to catch some of the rainwater. He said that the ship's drinking water had been taken from the Savannah River which was "thick & muddy," and the rainwater was a welcome relief.

At six in the evening the *Taylor* grounded in the mud. There was nothing Anderson or the crew could do but wait for high tide to help them off. It was 4:00 A.M. before the ship was free to steam on. At 8:00 A.M. she anchored off Jacksonville, where she remained for a day because of the gale winds blowing from the southwest. Anderson noted that Jacksonville had about six hundred people and was "one bed of heavy sand."[11]

Around 1845 the Savannah Line began regular operations between Savannah and the St. Johns. Initially the line had three ships: *Ocmulgee*, *St. Matthews*, and *William Gaston*. In 1851 the *Welaka* and *Magnolia* were added to the fleet. The Savannah Line was dogged by misfortune. In 1854 the *Gaston* was sold and became a river boat. The *Magnolia*'s boiler exploded off St. Simons Island, killing Captain William T. McNelty. Later the *Welaka* was wrecked on the St. Johns Bar. The *Seminole* and *St. Johns* replaced these last two vessels. Both replacements caught fire and burned at their docks in Jacksonville. The hull of the *St. Johns* was raised and rebuilt, and she continued on the same route until 1862. After the Civil War she was renamed the *Helen Getty*. The last vessel of the Savannah Line was the *St. Marys*, acquired in 1857.[12]

Jacob Brock, a Vermonter, was among the early steamboat captains on the St. Johns. He recognized the tourist trade's potential. He was the owner of the *Darlington*, a western river-type vessel whose main deck was cluttered with freight surrounding the ship's engine. The *Darlington* was a South Carolina-built vessel completed in 1849. She spent her first years on the Pedee River traveling into the Darlington District, whence she got her name. Brock acquired her in 1852 to use between Jacksonville and his Brock House at Enterprise. Brock set aside a small salon for women and children to protect them from the vulgarity of the Grand Salon, although the latter served as the dining room at mealtimes.[13]

There were two navigational approaches to Jacksonville: the inland passage, which was restricted to small vessels, and the ocean route, through the shifting channel over the bar at the mouth of the river. Dr. Abel Seymour Baldwin was the first man to seriously study this problem of the moving channel of the St. Johns. Until Baldwin provided an answer to the question of why the river bed did not remain in one place, no one had given it much thought. From his study, he concluded that the Fort George Inlet was the culprit. Normally, the sediment, carried down a river by the current, fans out and settles when the river flows into the ocean, where its current is diffused in the larger body of water. This is part of the creation of shoal waters about the mouth of a river. However, the main current from the river, continuing its force longer, has the effect of cutting through the shoal grounds, creating the channel of the river bed.

Dr. Baldwin determined that the opening of Fort George Inlet, no more than a mile or two north of the St. Johns, under certain circumstances of tide and current, had an injurious effect upon the main channel. During each tide there was an interchange of waters between the river and the inlet, brought about because of the different time of the flood and ebb tides in each outlet. Fort George Inlet flooded anywhere from one and a half to three hours before the ebb current of the St. Johns River stopped flowing over the bar. During this period, a large volume of water passing out the river's mouth was pulled northward into the inlet. Thus, a series of swash channels over the north shoal were formed, which diminished the amount, velocity, and force of the waters flowing out the St. Johns River's main channel.[14]

He also noted that local wind conditions contributed to the uniqueness of the St. Johns Bar. Prevalent northeasterly winds pushed the river waters back up the St. Johns, causing a decrease in the volume and velocity of the waters in the main channel. The result was that the sand thrown up by the ocean waves met a reduced ebb flow and it was deposited in large amounts in the channel, further shallowing the depth of the bar. The reverse was true from prolonged westerly winds. The ebb current was increased by the wind push, causing a greater depth of water over the bar.[15]

Still another factor was the littoral current. The average storm flow (littoral current) of the Atlantic Ocean along the Florida coast was in a southern direction, and the sand from the littoral current washed southward along the coast until it came in contact with river or inlet currents moving eastward. When this occurred, the sand was deposited on the upflow side of the intersection of the littoral and the river current, building a sand bar on the north side of the outflow. The river current, seeking the path of least resistance, swung southward, closely followed by an ever-building curved sand bar. In cases where the inlet flow was weak, the littoral current would seal shut the exit to the ocean. On the other hand, strong river currents would bend southward three or four thousand feet from the original track.[16]

The St. Johns channel, over time, would swing gradually south until conditions were such that the river current would punch another channel through the shoals in a more easterly direction. The southern channel would fill up with sediment again. At times, the St. Johns would have two main cuts to the ocean; at other times, it had only a northern or a southern deep-water exit. Is it any wonder that throughout the years the sinuous channel challenged the coastal captains calling upon the port of Jacksonville?

All of these phenomena added to the risks a merchantman encountered using the St. Johns River. Smaller ships, which were safe enough in draft, often were too light to be seaworthy in the Atlantic, especially during the fall hurricane season; large ocean vessels might stand off the bar for days or weeks waiting to enter the river. Once over the bar, the route to Jacksonville was relatively easy. With added cargo, the ship might have to wait once again for enough water to exit the St. Johns. Jacksonville, as a seaport, competed poorly against Fernandina and Savannah, even though it drew upon the tremendous resources of the St. Johns valley.

The early solution to the shifting channel, and the one promoted by the people at Fernandina on Amelia Island, was to use their deep-water harbor. Small coastal steamers could steam from Jacksonville to Fernandina by either the protected intracoastal waterway or the outer oceanway, where the goods could be transferred to the larger vessels for any destinations bordering the world's seas. This was not acceptable, however, to Dr. Baldwin or the citizens of Jacksonville, who dreamed of opening the St. Johns River so that their own city might engage in world trade.

Baldwin presented his answer to the shifting channel in 1852 when he suggested closing up the Fort George Inlet. He reasoned that the waters of the Fort George River then would be added to those of the St. Johns. Two effects would result: the elimination of the crosscurrent over the shoal ground; and the strengthening of the main flow of the St. Johns River, which would aid in the creation and deepening of the cut across the shoal grounds. The logic of his observations resulted in the town's voting to send Baldwin to Washington, D.C., to present his proposal before Congress to seek federal aid.

At first, everything went as planned. Florida representatives presented the doctor's views to Congress, and received permission for him to explain his project to the Topographical Bureau. The bureau accepted and approved of his plan with a recommendation to Congress to appropriate money to carry out the project. Congress provided twenty thousand dollars.

Unfortunately for Dr. Baldwin and Jacksonville, Congress failed to pass a bill for fortifications that session; therefore, the funds appropriated in the Lighthouse Bill and River and Harbor Bill were divided between the Corps of Engineers and the Topographical Corps. This resulted in works on the Atlantic being assigned to the Corps of Engineers, while the Topographical Corps received the projects on the Great Lakes and western rivers. Dr. Baldwin had to start over again with the Corps of Engineers.

In his dealings with the Corps he related: "I at once called upon the chief of the Military Bureau, General [Joseph G.] Totten, and offered to give him a history and exposition of my plan, but his time was too much occupied in assigning the work in various localities to the charge of separate engineers to listen to me. I was requested to leave any statement in writing, or confer with the engineer in whose charge the work would be placed."[17] The doctor left Washington to await the results of his efforts.

The next winter, Lieutenant Horatio Wright arrived in Jacksonville to study plans for the improvement of the St. Johns channel. When Wright informed the doctor that the original funds from Congress were paying for the survey, Dr. Baldwin immediately objected. According to his interpretation, Congress had accepted his proposal and the monies were appropriated to close Fort George Inlet, but his protest was to no avail. This was the beginning of a running feud between Dr. Baldwin and the Corps which was to last over a quarter of a century.

When Wright recommended the construction of a single pier on the north bank of the outer channel, Baldwin was convinced that the Corps of Engineers was out to destroy his scheme. He knew the cost of a pier was above the limit Congress could reasonably expect to finance. Further, the doctor was sure that a pier would not change his original premise. It would project the channel farther out to sea, but when the pier ended, the same influences from Fort George would be there to act as always. He believed that Lieutenant Wright was wrong.

Ultimately, the support of the local population for Dr. Baldwin and the extreme difference in the solutions proposed by the doctor and the lieutenant led the Chief Engineer to refer the problem to a special commission, consisting of a navy captain, a captain and two lieutenants from the Corps of Engineers, and a civilian. Lt. Wright and Dr. Baldwin both were on the commission. The result was two statements: a majority report subscribed to by the government officers, and a minority statement signed by Dr. Baldwin. Lt. Wright was right.

The formal hearing did not end Dr. Baldwin's fight with the Corps. In 1857, he obtained another examination of the mouth and bar of the St. Johns, this time under the direction of Lieutenant Stephen D. Trenchard, USN, who was serving with the Coast Survey Service. Dr. Baldwin was delighted with the results. A comparison of the 1853 and 1857 charts showed great changes in the underwater topography, which convinced the doctor that his assumptions had been justified.[18] But once again, Dr. Baldwin's goal was thwarted, this time by the outbreak of a major conflict—the Civil War.

Chapter Seven

THE BLOCKADE

The twelfth of April 1861, the day Confederate forces bombarded Fort Sumter, began in Jacksonville the same as most days after the withdrawal of the Southern States from the Union. Locally the paper wrote of the construction of several new wharves in town which would strengthen port facilities. Then word of the firing on Fort Sumter began to come in over the telegraph wires from Savannah. Before amplifications could be sent, the wires went dead, leaving the people in Jacksonville wondering what had happened. The next day the Steamer *Cecile* arrived from Charleston with eyewitness accounts of the opening of hostilities.[1]

Confederate President Jefferson Davis faced the task of creating a navy. In his April 1861 proclamation, he called for letters of marque hoping to entice adventurers to the profits of privateering. Louis M. Coxetter, a popular St. Johns River captain, accepted Davis's call. He became a privateer commanding the *Jeff Davis* (the former slaver *Echo*), a five-gun, seventy-four man brig of 230 tons. On a seven-week cruise during July and August 1861, from Maine to Delaware, he captured nine merchantmen. At one time, there were eight Union Navy ships assigned to run him down. He headed for St. Augustine, where he had to wait two days for a gale to blow over. Then going in, he grounded, losing his brig. When he and his crew arrived in Jacksonville after his disaster, the whole town turned out to welcome the privateers and to celebrate their victories. Had the Confederacy had more privateers like Coxetter, the Union blockade might have been less effective and naval operations might have developed differently.[2]

Although President Davis counted on actions such as Coxetter performed to be part of the South's answer to the North's naval power, he could not foresee Europe's reaction. Both England and France refused to allow prize courts within their sovereignties. As the blockade became effective, it became difficult to bring prizes into Southern ports. Finally, and probably more telling, seafaring adventurers found higher profits and less danger acting as blockade-runners rather than as privateers. The end result was that the Confederacy only sent out about thirty privateers, and most of these vessels were small, poorly armed, and inadequate for the task. When Coxetter tried to outfit a new privateering expedition, he failed to receive any backing; therefore, he settled for command of the steamer *Herald*, and became a blockage-runner. He added to his fame as a blockade-runner, but he was no longer in the business of destroying enemy merchantmen.[3]

It took time for the Union Navy to create an effective blockade for the port of Jacksonville. But with the outbreak of hostilities, many of the steamer captains plying the river turned immediately to blockade-running. Captain Jacob Brock had the distinction of bringing the first shipment into Jacksonville after the blockade had been proclaimed. He brought his *Darlington* loaded with provisions up to Cyrus Bisbee's wharf. Both men were New Englanders devoted to the Southern cause. The *Cecile* and the *Kate* made numerous runs before they were wrecked in 1862. The *St. Johns* and the *St. Marys*, two Savannah steamers, ran the blockade many times, occasionally coming into Jacksonville.[4]

Near the end of October 1861, the yacht *Camilla* from England crossed the St. Johns Bar, bearing dispatches for the Confederate government. Her lines gave her away, and word spread throughout Jacksonville that the famous yacht *America*, winner of the "America's Cup," had crossed the blockade. She made at least two trips from Jacksonville, but as the blockade tightened, the risks of capture became greater. Her last run through the blockade into Jacksonville was made in March 1862.[5]

The blockaders gradually tightened their hold over Jacksonville, as a series of captures of blockade-runners demonstrate. On 12 October 1861, the USS *Dale* took possession of the outward-bound schooner *Specie* just to the east of the St. Johns. She had a cargo of rice for the Havana market. A month later, the *Dale* captured the blockade-runner *Mabel*, of recent British registry, formerly the *John W. Anderson* of Baltimore, to the east of Jacksonville.[6]

On 11 December 1861, as Commander Charles Steedman, of the USS *Bienville*, steamed southward along the coast toward the St. Johns Bar, he sighted two sails. He immediately gave chase. When almost upon them the crew of the pilot-boat schooner abandoned her and went aboard the other vessel. Steedman continued the chase, driving the blockade-runner onto the breakers at the mouth of the St. Johns. However, he deemed it too dangerous to continue, with night falling. Steedman returned to the first schooner, which proved to be the *Sarah and Caroline* from Jacksonville, Charles Brown her master. Among the letters aboard the ship was one from a son in Jacksonville to his mother which said in part that "quite a little trade sprung up between this place [Jacksonville] and the same island [in the Bahamas] . . . But don't blab, for if Seward should hear of it he would put Lincoln up to send a blockading vessel to stop it."[7]

Two weeks later, Steedman, cruising off the St. Johns River, noted a schooner standing off to land. He closed with and captured the *Arrow* carrying a load of salt. The next day, while anchored in nine fathoms of water, two and a half miles east of the St. Johns Bar, Steedman saw a schooner to landward trying to enter the river. He shipped his anchor and began his chase. He fired several shots at the vessel before she gave up attempting to escape. As she bore up and ran down to the *Bienville*, she displayed English colors. But on boarding the prize, she turned out to be the *Alert*, whose master and owner was a citizen of Savannah. Steedman put aboard a prize crew to take the blockade-runner and her crew to Philadelphia for adjudication.[8] So in a matter of months the navy was on station off the Confederate coast. Although the vessels were not always in sight, the people on shore knew of the blockaders' presence.

The Blockade Strategy Board meeting in June 1861, under the chairmanship of Captain Samuel F. DuPont, recommended a series of amphibious operations to seize vital bases on the Confederate coastline to be used for supply, repair, and recreation bases for the blockading squadrons, and as staging areas by the army for operations into the enemy's hinterland. The Board's broad policies were accepted and carried out throughout the course of the war. This led to DuPont's promotion to flag officer, and he commanded the South Atlantic Blockading Squadron when it captured Port Royal and Hilton Head, South Carolina. His next step was to secure a base in northeast Florida.[9]

Following the capture of Port Royal, a stream of Union supporters and contrabands slipped through the lines to this Northern enclave with military information about northeast Florida from the Cumberland Sound to St. Augustine. Dr. Henry Balsam, founder of New Berlin on the St. Johns River just downstream from Jacksonville, and Isaac Tatnall, an escaped slave who had been the pilot of the steamer *St. Marys*, were among the informants. These men provided information on Confederate defenses and local navigation which was instrumental in DuPont's decision to capture Fernandina.[10]

While DuPont gathered information on northeast Florida, Captain Charles Willey, now residing in Jacksonville, and the owner of the *Rebecca*, prepared his ship to run the blockade. She left Jacksonville on 3 February 1862, but had to remain in Mayport until 2 March waiting for tide, weather, and the absence of Union blockaders before venturing into the Atlantic. She carried turpentine and resin on her outward voyage. The *Rebecca* probably was the last blockade-runner to leave from the mouth of the St. Johns River.[11]

Meanwhile, as a part of General Robert E. Lee's policy of consolidating military defenses until the North had committed itself, General James H. Traiper received orders to evacuate Fernandina, on Amelia island, and Cumberland island. This happened just four days before DuPont sailed from Port Royal for northeast Florida. Traiper's evacuation was still in process when the Union Fleet appeared.

As DuPont arrived in Fernandina, an escaped slave rowed out with the news that the Confederates were fleeing by rail. DuPont ordered his shallow-draft gunboats to push ahead to destroy the rail trestle linking Fernandina with the mainland. Only the USS *Ottawa* reached the Amelia River in time, and a bizarre chase took place between the Confederate soldiers on the train pursued by Union sailors in a gunboat. For a two mile stretch the tracks ran parallel to the river. Passengers and soldiers began firing upon the *Ottawa*, and the ship's guns returned fire. Two young men sat on a sofa on the last railroad car, which was loaded with furniture and bedding. They were hanging on, enjoying the chase, when a shell from the *Ottawa* burst over the last car, killing them instantly and scattering furniture in all directions. Trainmen quickly released the damaged car, allowing the train to continue on over the bridge to the mainland and safety.[12]

While the train-gunboat race was underway, another chase was setting up. In Fernandina, Captain Jacob Brock loaded his *Darlington* with military supplies, wagons, mules, forage, and as many women and children as he could carry, and, while the Federals were concerned with the fleeing train, he headed for a small creek which flowed under the same railroad bridge. He knew that the *Ottawa* could not go up that creek. But Commander C. R. P. Rogers took two armed launches in full pursuit after Brock. Only when all means of escape had eluded him did Brock surrender. Afterwards, DuPont reported that "the brutal captain [Brock] suffered her [the *Darlington*] to be fired upon and refused to hoist a white flag, notwithstanding the entreaties of the women. No one was injured." He also told Secretary of the Navy Welles that: "We captured Port Royal, but Fernandina and Fort Clinch have been given to us."[13]

Later DuPont sent gunboats south into the St. Johns River as far as Jacksonville. By the time of the Federal invasion of the river, the pro-Northerners of Jacksonville were beside themselves with joy at their expected liberation. But after crossing the bar, the United States ships stopped at the mouth of the river to discharge a detachment of soldiers to secure the entrance before moving up to Jacksonville; the delay was nerve-racking for the town's Unionists.

On 11 March 1862, Jacksonville was defenseless. The only Confederate troops left were there to burn public property before the Northerners arrived. They put the torch to seven steam sawmills, much lumber, an iron foundry, and a partially built gunboat. The soldiers of the rear guard were careful not to damage private property, and Union sympathizers were relieved, for many had feared that the troops might punish them for their Federal allegiance. However, about midnight, as the Confederate soldiers departed, and before the Union troops arrived, Florida irregulars moved into town and began intimidating the Unionists. At least three Northern men were shot in the streets or as they fled to boats headed downriver for the protection of Federal guns. Indiscriminate shooting broke out, some fires were set, and soon there was mass panic in Jacksonville. Many of the Unionists fled across the river to hide on the south bank until Federal forces arrived.[14]

Thus did the outside blockade come to Jacksonville. Although the Union Army occupied and left the city on three different occasions before the fourth and final occupation, the navy was on the river to stay. Hence forth Confederate ships running the blockade would have to find other outlets; the mouth of the St. Johns River was closed to the South.

Chapter Eight

THE INNER BLOCKADE

Navy gunboats steaming up and down the St. Johns River created an inner blockade which was more detrimental to Florida's
military effort than the outer blockade. When the mouth of the
river closed, Floridians carried their cotton upriver and overland
to the Mosquito Lagoon or to the Indian River to be shipped
through the offshore blockade. But the inner blockade disrupted
this traffic. It also separated St. Augustine and the lower east
bank of the river from the rest of the Confederacy, creating a haven for Unionists, contrabands, and, as time went on, for the
war weary.

Influential citizens of Jacksonville made preparations to protect their blockade-runners from the advancing Northerners.
Colonel J. C. Hemming was assigned to take the steamer *St.
Marys* and the yacht *America* upriver to be scuttled in some tributary well away from Federal discovery. Hemming turned into
Dunn's Creek, where the keel of the yacht kept it from progress-
ing too far upstream. He scuttled her in three fathoms of water,
with only the port rail showing above the surface. Then he proceeded farther with the *St. Marys*, crossing Dunn's Lake and entering Haw Creek. Here the steamer was allowed to settle on the
muddy bottom to await a more opportune time to work for the
Confederate cause.

The Federals did not plan to occupy Jacksonville when they arrived in March 1862. They were conducting a reconnaissance mission, but Unionists pleaded with the commanders to remain to ensure their safety. The result was that the Northern troops moved ashore and built defenses around Jacksonville.

While the troops were being off-loaded, Lt. Thomas H. Stevens, commander of the gunboat *Ottawa*, boarded the steamer *Ellen*, a lighter draft vessel than his own, to steam upriver on a survey of the territory. At Palatka he met a person who told him that the Confederates had taken the *St. Marys* and the *America* up one of the river's tributaries to hide them. The informant only knew vaguely where the ships were located. On Stevens's return trip, he came upon a small boat with two people in it. As he turned his steamer toward them, they rowed frantically for shore, where they jumped into the shallow water, splashed into the underbrush and escaped capture. However, when Stevens examined the boat, he found a letter from Colonel J. C. Hemming giving complete directions as to the whereabouts of the scuttled vessels.

Stevens returned to Jacksonville to organize salvage operations. The next day he left in the *Darlington*, the *Ellen*, and two launches from the *Wabash* to claim his prizes. At Dunn's Creek he found the yacht. Leaving the *Ellen* on guard, he pushed on through Dunn's Lake to Haw Creek, where he found the *St. Marys*. Unfortunately for Stevens, he had to return to Jacksonville for additional equipment to raise the ships. Then he worked his sailors for a week to refloat the *America*. Later, the navy refitted her for duty with the squadron off Charleston.

Unknown to Stevens and his sailors, Captain Winston Stephens, with some of his men of the Second Florida Cavalry, watched the whole operation. Captain Stephens was there to prevent the capture of the *America*, but, in his own words: "I can't shoot them. I just can't do it—it would be murder."[1] He returned to his base at Welaka.

Lt. Stevens did not have the opportunity to return to raise the *St. Marys*, as other duties on the lower river kept him busy. Later the Confederates were the ones to refloat the St. Marys and return her to clandestine operations on the St. Johns, where she sometimes steamed as far north as Jacksonville.

Meanwhile, DuPont also sent gunboats south to St. Augustine. On 11 March 1862, Commander C. R. P. Rodgers of the frigate *Wabash* anchored off the mouth of St. Augustine's harbor. The day before, Confederate soldiers, accompanied by a number of the town's civilians, had left for the interior. Mayor Christobal Bravo raised the white flag over Fort Marion, whereupon Rodgers boarded a small boat and went to the town's wharf where he met the mayor in the midst of a crowd of curious onlookers. The two officials went to the town hall, where the council was in session. Here Rodgers conducted the formal ceremony of surrender.[2]

A week later Lt. J. W. A. Nicholson, commanding the *Isaac Smith*, entered St. Augustine harbor with a marine battalion augmented by an army company of the Seventh New Hampshire Regiment. On 3 April Nicholson heard that a schooner had crossed the Matanzas Bar. He borrowed twenty-five army men to accompany him in three armed boats when he headed south to investigate. He captured the blockade-runner *Empire City*, of English registry, cleared from Nassau for St. John, New Brunswick. However, on closer examination of the crew only the captain had escaped; Nicholson learned that she was Captain Willey's *Rebecca* returning with provisions, dry goods, and medicines. The last vessel to run the blockade from Jacksonville became entrapped upon its return.

Often the contraband (a term used to refer to any Southern black man within Northern lines) provided valuable services as a pilot or guide. The escaped slave was in a more dangerous position on these expeditions into the interior because the enemy showed little mercy toward a captured contraband. The black pilot on the USS *Penguin* is a case in point. In late March 1862 Federal authorities received word of an arms shipment arriving in Mosquito Inlet. Lieutenant Thomas A. Budd of the *Penguin* and Acting Master S. W. Mather of the *Henry Andrew* went to investigate.

Budd organized an expedition of four or five boats, with crews from both vessels to scour the shore. Both commanding officers went on the search. Budd took the inland passage and proceeded fifteen to eighteen miles south of New Smyrna before giving up. On the return the boats became strung out. Budd decided to investigate some abandoned earthworks in the dense underbrush. Just as he neared shore, heavy fire poured in from the cover, killing Budd, Mather, and two sailors instantly. Two others were seriously injured and the black pilot had a slight wound in his foot. All were captured. The remaining boats, under fire, retreated to the opposite bank, where the sailors hid in the underbrush. At dusk, an acting master's mate gathered the men, returned to the boats, and, passing close by the rebel pickets, made good his escape.

Flag Officer DuPont arrived off Mosquito Inlet as the men returned, and he ordered extra boats to cross the bar that night. The next morning the navy had a substantial group inside the bay, but no enemy could be found. Later, under a flag of truce, the bodies of Budd and Mather were returned. The black pilot had been summarily hanged shortly after his capture.

Sometime afterwards, Lt. Daniel Ammen picked up six contrabands on the St. Johns. Three of the men claimed that their master was George Huston, a captain in the Florida militia, who had built a boom across Black Creek, and placed coverts nearby, where his men might shoot at any sailors moving up the creek. One of Huston's slaves shipped on as a pilot and guide. This man told Ammen that his ex-master had participated in the *Penguin-Henry Andrew* skirmish at New Smyrna. He insisted that Huston had been the one demanding the hanging of the captured black pilot. He also said that Huston led regulators against the Unionists living along the St. Johns. Ammen decided he must capture and remove Huston from the local scene.

Ammen's lieutenant arrived at Huston's house about daybreak. Huston, forewarned, met him at the door heavily armed.

When the lieutenant demanded his surrender, Huston drew his pistol and mortally shot the officer. The sailors immediately returned his fire, and Huston fell with four serious wounds. The blockaders carried him back to their ship. Two months after the affair, George Huston died of his wounds aboard the gunboat; his body was returned to his widow.[3]

Often contrabands identified enemy prisoners. Ammen captured Durham Hall while he was being rowed across the St. Johns River. Hall was a member of the Florida militia, and his commanding general desired to set up an exchange for him. Ammen refused, claiming that Hall was captured in civilian clothes "not as a soldier but as a disturber of the public peace."[4] The slave who had been rowing Hall joined Ammen's crew, and he convinced Ammen that Hall was another regulator terrorizing the Unionists along the river. Ammen placed Hall in double irons; later, he said that Hall's capture had decreased the threats directed to Union sympathizers within the area of his patrol.

On 24 March 1862, Jacksonville's Unionists felt secure enough under Federal troops to announce a convention of loyalists to meet in a month's time to create a state government under the Union. Unexpectedly, just before the convention, the Federal Army received orders to evacuate Jacksonville. The Unionists were dumbfounded. They had openly declared themselves for the Union. They could no longer remain in their homes. Despite their pleading, the army could do no better than to offer the Unionists transportation to Fernandina or St. Augustine.

Although the army withdrew from Jacksonville, Flag Officer DuPont left some of his gunboats at Mayport. He reasoned that it took fewer ships to blockade the river when stationed at its mouth than it would if his ships were on station at sea beyond the bar. Further, the winter storms would endanger, and occasionally drive off, his ships at sea, weakening the blockade. But ships at the mouth of the river could maintain a tighter blockade under safer conditions. DuPont opted to create a series of inner blockades along his squadron's coast at "St. Catherine's, Sapelo, Doboy, and St. Simon's sounds, Fernandina, St. John's River, St.

Augustine, and Mosquito Inlet, thus closing the entire coast of Florida and Georgia to all efforts of the rebels and our neutral friends to introduce provisions or arms."[5]

After the gunboats began patrolling the river, many people sought safety with the blockaders. In early June 1862, Lt. Ammen picked up a Northern lady and a Confederate soldier who had deserted. A few weeks later, Lt. Nicholson took aboard the Myers and Tombs families, seventeen people. Both families fled to the navy because they had been ordered to move into the interior.[6]

The Confederate reaction to the navy's patrols was to order all residents living on the banks of the river who were suspected of disloyalty to move inland ten miles. It also destroyed small boats along the banks so that dissidents would not be able to communicate with the enemy forces afloat.[7]

The blockaders, too, were eliminating boats along the St. Johns. Commander Maxwell Woodhull wrote of destroying "perhaps a thousand boats. They were so numerous on our first appearance in the river it might almost be said to be 'bridged over.' " He did this to keep the Confederate regular and guerrilla forces from crossing to the eastern shore to bother Unionists. Of course, navy ships carried oared boats, enabling the blockaders to communicate with individuals on shore at will.[8]

The destruction of small boats along the St. Johns River was detrimental to the Southerners because it destroyed their means of crossing the river. Later, when the Confederates executed raids on the east bank, horses and wagons were ferried over on unwieldy rafts. Such an awkward craft, if caught in midstream, would be extremely vulnerable to the blockaders' gunboats.

On 7 April 1862, Governor John Milton wrote to President Jefferson Davis that the retirement of Confederate forces from Fernandina and the St. Johns River had demoralized many of the Florida troops and it had a serious impact upon the citizenry. He said that as soon as he could, he would declare Florida east of the St. Johns to be under martial law, because so many citizens had already demonstrated that they were ready to submit to the enemy at the first opportunity.[9]

A few days later, General Richard F. Floyd, the Confederate commander of the state troops, received from Captain J. W. Pearson of the Oklawaha Rangers firsthand information on East Florida. "At least three-fourths of the people on the St. Johns River and east of it are aiding and abetting the enemy; we could see them at all times through the day communicating with the vessel in their small boats." Pearson went on: "It is not safe for a small force to be on the east side of the river; there is great danger of being betrayed into the hands of the enemy."[10] He said that he had two or three men already marked for hanging.

General Floyd wrote to the governor on 11 April suggesting that the eastern counties be placed under martial law as they "contain a nest of traitors and lawless negroes." Just as soon as he had sufficient units he would move in, for "thus far treason has boldly appeared in our midst with impunity; the hour to deal with it summarily has arrived."[11] Unfortunately for both the governor and the general, the military situation was not such that they could deal with it promptly or effectively.

A few days after Captain Pearson wrote to General Floyd, he took his men to the east bank near Orange Mills to ambush a Union detachment expected to arrive momentarily. Pearson made his crossing at night to secure secrecy. By dawn some of his men were still on the west bank. Pearson hid, waiting for darkness, when the rest of his men could join him. But just at dusk, a gunboat hove in sight and anchored about four miles below the mills. The captain decided that, in the face of a Union gunboat, it was useless to attempt a surprise attack with only a portion of his men. He remained hidden until the next night, when he recrossed the river. By early Monday morning Pearson and his men were seven miles inland from Palatka, heading back to camp.

F. L. Dancy, who gave Pearson the information about the Union troops' move to Orange Mills, stated: "I am convinced [the ambush] failed through information furnished them by traitors living in our midst and communicating with the enemy with impunity by means of boats and otherwise. There were not less than four boats from different points on the river that communicated with the propeller [the gunboat] during Sunday."[12]

Lt. Ammen cruised the waters of the St. Johns, picking up Unionists, contrabands, and Confederate deserters. He also talked to people on shore. From bits of conversations he began to suspect that the Confederates had been using steamers in spite of the navy's control of the river. He heard that the *Silver Springs* and the *Governor Milton* were seen on Black Creek, a tributary too shallow for his gunboat, just south of Jacksonville.

Ammen's suspicions were correct. Confederate General Joseph Finegan searched the area for guns to use against the navy. In Volusia he found two eight-inch Columbiads, which he moved to Black Creek by steamer without being detected by the navy gunboats. Because he knew that there were Unionists living along the river who would inform the navy of these movements, he ordered all suspected people to move inland ten miles so that he could cloak his actions from prying eyes.[13]

Not all Unionists moved. When the Browards told Dr. Henry Balsam to move, he sought protection from Lt. Nicholson, who told him to return to his house at Dames Point and to shoot anyone prowling about. That night after dark, Nicholson sent the *Uncas* up to Dames Point with instructions to shell the woods surrounding Balsam's place. The next day, Nicholson moved up river to shell the Broward house, which flushed out a party of eight mounted men who fled into the woods.[14]

In August General Finegan sent soldiers to St. Johns Bluff to prepare the terrain for the guns he had gathered outside of Jacksonville. By the first of September, Finegan knew time was running out for him to execute his plan, for Master L. C. Crane, of the *Uncas*, on a trip upriver from the Navy anchorage at Mayport Mills, noted the activity of the soldiers on the bluff. He fired several shots among the soldiers and was satisfied that he had routed them.

Finegan ordered Captain Winston Stephens to attack Mayport Mills to keep the sailors and their gunboats busy while he armed St. Johns Bluff. Stephens hit the settlement on the night of 6 September, and managed to set fire to one house before being driven off by the sailors.

Meanwhile, Finegan moved all the guns he had collected on rafts, towed by the *Governor Milton,* from Jacksonville to St. Johns Bluff between 6 and 9 September without being detected. Unfortunately for Finegan, Israel, a slave living in western Jacksonville, fled to Mayport Mills to report what the general was doing. Master Crane steamed up to the bluffs on the night of 10 September to lob a few shells into the area. Captain Joseph L. Dunham, the Confederate in charge at the time, refrained from answering because he knew that the powder flashes would give away his gun positions. But at daybreak, when he could see the *Uncas* clearly, he opened up on the anchored gunboat. The *Uncas* was hit five times before she slipped her anchor and got underway. In spite of the hits registered on the ship, none of the crew suffered injury. Crane returned fire for an hour as the two sides shelled each other. Once his ship was in motion, it was not hit by enemy fire. General Finegan claimed victory for this engagement.[15]

When Admiral DuPont heard of this activity, and of Finegan's challenge to his squadron, he sent three ships to boost the Navy's firepower at the mouth of the St. Johns.[16] The next gun duel, which lasted five hours, was between seven gunboats and the batteries on the bluff, and was clearly a standoff; neither side suffered grievous losses. Commander Charles Steedman wrote to DuPont that it would take a combined operation to wrest St. Johns Bluff from the rebels.

DuPont concurred. General John Milton Brannan was selected to lead the troops dispatched to take the bluff. On 1 October the soldiers were off-loaded at Mayport Mills and the next day they began their trek through the swamps and woods to capture the bluff. Lieutenant Colonel Charles F. Hopkins, now commanding at St. Johns Bluff, told General Finegan that the Yankees had landed three thousand troops. Later Hopkins revised his figures upward to five thousand attackers. In truth, Brannan had fifteen hundred soldiers.

Quite unexpectedly Colonel Hopkins decided to withdraw before the first Yankee arrived. He pulled his forces out at night without being detected. The next morning, while the troops were struggling through the underbrush toward the bluff, the gunboats sent some shells crashing into the rebel gun emplacements which did not elicit any reply. The sailors went ashore to find the bluff deserted, with the guns primed and loaded. Thus, when the soldiers arrived at the top of the bluff, they were met by sailors who had raised the Stars and Stripes over the emplacements.[17]

The second occupation of Jacksonville followed the capture of St. Johns Bluff. It was not intended to be a permanent takeover. Troops were in Jacksonville for four days for the express purpose of ensuring that other fortifications had not been built to challenge the U.S. Navy as it patrolled the river.

The small coastal steamer *Darlington,* one of the prizes taken when Fernandina was captured, became an army transport. The navy provided a contraband crew who knew the local waters. Commander Percival Drayton left instructions for his relief concerning the precautions he employed on the *Darlington* because of her contraband crew. Normally, when she went out on an expedition beyond local waters, he put an officer, an engineer, and ten to forty armed men aboard to protect the crew.[18] The *Darlington* participated in the second occupation of Jacksonville.

A contraband former pilot of the rebel steamer *Governor Milton* came over to the Union with information on the whereabouts of the steamer. He offered to lead an expedition for its capture. The navy, anxious to seize the *Governor Milton* for its part in the rearming of the St. Johns Bluff, accepted his offer. The *Darlington* and the *E. B. Hale,* both shallow-draft, steamed upriver for the prize. The *Hale* had to anchor at the mouth of the Oklawaha River because of its draft. The *Darlington* pushed on. At Hawkinsville the crew found traces of the *Milton's* recent departure up one of the smaller creeks too shallow even for the *Darlington.* The crew manned boats to continue the chase. A few miles farther upcreek they found the *Milton* tied to the bank with two engineers on board. They took possession of the steamer, fired her up, and searched upcreek a little way before returning to the two Union ships waiting for them.[19]

Acting Master Edward McKeige wrote that, since his arrival at Mayport Mills, five or six families had moved to Batton Island, on the opposite bank, The island had long been the residence of bar pilots of the St. Johns River. It was connected to Fort George Island by a wooden bridge sixty feet long. The pilots fled to the woods earlier to live in shanties under great fear of the Confederates because of their loyalty to, and the services they rendered to, the U.S. Navy. McKeige destroyed the bridge, cutting off communications with Fort George Island, thus isolating Batton Island from Confederate marauders. Many of the bar pilots returned to their homes just as soon as the bridge was destroyed.[20] After the pilots moved back to Pilot Town, a permanent settlement of Union sympathizers grew up there.

By early November, Commander Woodhull reported a nucleus of five men, three women, and a half dozen children at Pilot Town. Near the end of the month the population had grown to nearly a hundred, black and white. Most of the people fleeing to the Union were destitute. Many left everything, setting out at night in small boats with a few belongings. Woodhull furnished the refugees with rations, and sometimes even clothing. His major solicitude was food. By December he was feeding a hundred civilians as well as his own squadron, and he was down to fifteen or twenty days' supply. But he felt this was worth it, for "if the colony is broken up, we will lose the advantage of this nucleus for them to rally around, who might otherwise be compelled to give their services to the rebels."[21]

The commander saw the advantages of this refugee colony. His talks with those at Pilot Town convinced him that "there are numbers of others that will join us as soon as circumstances will permit them to escape."[22] Every fresh arrival reported the same story of the increase of desertions among the Florida troops and the great dissatisfaction with the conduct of the war. Woodhull commented that "the people along the river bank are well disposed to us, and I am satisfied from their conversation that they are very tired of the war; that discontent and discouragement are very prevalent among the masses."[23]

By now there were enough men at Pilot Town for Woodhull to organize them into semi-military units to provide their own guards for the colony. As further protection, Woodhull built a heavy abatis, an obstacle for defense consisting of embedded sharpened tree trunks, which he placed in the creek bottoms from Cedar Point to Trout Creek to keep marauding rebel bands on the mainland from approaching Pilot Town in small boats. Yet, in spite of all these precautions, Woodhull strongly recommended that the army establish a post near the refugee camp to give confidence to these people that they were safe from recapture. If that happened, "there would be a rapid melting away of the armed men composing the whole military strength of this part of Florida."[24]

DuPont also was concerned with this problem. Earlier he had written to the army's Department of the South that the navy had sixty contrabands on North Island, near Georgetown, Georgia, and almost a hundred refugees at Pilot Town. He requested instructions for their welfare. The army replied that it could take the contrabands immediately, but it had no place for the Pilot Town people until houses could be built at St. Helensville, South Carolina.[25] This was not what DuPont wanted. Moving Floridians to South Carolina would alienate many potential refugees. It was apparent that the army did not grasp the importance of the navy's contacts with Floridians.

Almost a year after Lt. Stevens had raised the *America*, Admiral DuPont received reports that the rebels had raised the *St. Marys*. According to his sources, the *St. Marys* and a small sternwheel tug were engaged in clandestine operations on the St. Johns River, sometimes as far north as Jacksonville. DuPont ordered Cdr. Steedman to take the *Norwich* and the *Uncas* upriver as far as necessary to confirm the status of the *St. Marys*. Two weeks later Steedman reported: "I have learned from reliable sources that there is no foundation for the report that the steamer

St. Marys has been raised or moved from the place where she was sunk some time ago."[26]

In the years after the Federal forces captured St. Johns Bluff, Jacksonville was occupied three times. It was burned twice, once by the Confederates when they withdrew, and at the end of the third occupation when the Federal troops left. But throughout that time the navy patrolled the St. Johns River, and St. Augustine remained in Union hands, serving as a rest camp for Federal forces. The United States made no major effort to extend its control over territory much beyond St. Augustine proper.

The question to be asked is, Why was St. Augustine so peaceful when protected by so few, especially when these troops made no effort to extend their control beyond the town limits? The answer is to be found in the navy's inner blockade. Those ships, based at Mayport Mills, made patrols as far upriver as Lake George. It was this inner blockade which limited Confederate activity on the east bank of the St. Johns River to a few hit-and-run expeditions. The danger of being trapped on the wrong side of the river by Union gunboats demanded caution.

In February 1864, just before the army occupied Jacksonville for the fourth and last time, Acting Master Frank B. Meriam, now commanding the *Norwich*, heard rumors that the *St. Marys* was in Jacksonville picking up cotton to carry upriver. The frequent reports upon the little Confederate steamer's operations seemed to defy and taunt the navy's river patrols. Meriam would like nothing better than to steam up to Jacksonville and destroy this rebel challenge to the inner blockade, but he could not jeopardize the army's operation.

When at last the soldiers embarked to make their surprise landing, Meriam and the *Norwich* were in the van. Meriam stood by while the troops disembarked. Then he immediately steamed to McGirt's Creek, on the outskirts of Jacksonville, to bottle up the *St. Marys*. The little steamer, loaded with bales of cotton, was trapped by the rapid occupation and could not steam up McGirt's Creek because of its draft. Meriam stationed a picket boat at the creek's entrance. The next morning he discovered the cotton had been burned and the ship scuttled, for the second time. The next time she was refloated, the Union Navy performed the work.[27]

The Department of the South's sudden interest in Florida stemmed from political reasons rather than military strategy. With the approach of a presidential election year, the Republican party expected to gain electoral votes if Florida could be occupied soon enough to bring another state into the political arena. Militarily, Florida now provided vital food to the Confederacy, so its occupation would hasten the conclusion of the war. The behind-the-scenes machinations which created the build up of Federal troops in Jacksonville are beyond the scope of this study; nevertheless, the end result was an increase in military strength in Florida by both sides, leading ultimately to the Battle of Olustee on 20 February 1864.[28] Olustee, the only major military engagement in the state throughout the war, was a Confederate victory. As the Union troops retreated to Jacksonville, it was the navy guns on the river which kept Jacksonville safe from the Confederate troops and provided the army with a safe haven from which to regroup.

Finally, in March 1864, the Confederates unleashed their latest weapon to clear gunboats from the St. Johns when they mined the river. (In their terminology, they employed torpedoes; however, these weapons were non-mobile charges of gunpowder sown in the river to explode when triggered by the blow of a passing ship.) The first inkling the navy had that mines were in the river occurred when the army transport *Maple Leaf*, on a trip from Palatka to Jacksonville at night, exploded one off Mandarin Point on 1 April 1864. In a matter of minutes she was on the bottom. Five crewmen, among the forty people aboard, were killed by the explosion. On 16 April, the second army transport, the *General Hunter*, hit a mine near where the first transport had gone down and lost one crewmember. Early in May a third transport, the *Harriet Weed*, steaming from Jacksonville toward the bar, struck two mines which lifted the vessel almost out of the water. The navy's reaction was to devise "torpedo catchers" to sweep over mine fields, cutting the mines from their moorings so that they would rise to the surface where they could be exploded.[29]

In spite of the challenge to the river's gunboats, the navy maintained its control over the St. Johns and its east bank. Drover Edwards, a landsman aboard the *Columbine* when she was captured by Captain J. J. Dickison of the Second Florida Cavalry, demonstrated the security of the east bank of the St. Johns. In May 1864 the *Columbine* had gone up to Volusia to check on the safety of the army detachments along the river. On her return, her captain, expecting to be fired upon by rebel infantry at Horse Landing, called all hands to quarters. During his approach he shelled the shore. Dickison, concealed on the west bank, waited until the ship was no more than thirty yards distant before he opened fire with several field pieces. The *Columbine*'s forward gun and wheel ropes were hit. Before the steering mechanism could be restored, she went aground to lay at Dickison's mercy. The skirmish lasted less than an hour. During that time both guns were put out of commission, and the carnage on deck caused Ensign Frank Sanborn to strike his colors.

Because no contraband could look forward to good treatment upon being captured, many of the black troops and seamen jumped in the river to try for the east bank, Edwards among them. He saw four black soldiers and a contraband shipmate, William Moran, sink below the waters. Later he came across three soldiers of the Thirty-fifth United States Colored Troops, and the four unarmed men made their way safely to St. Augustine, after a five-day trip through the wilderness.[30]

The eastern shore continued to be a safe haven for Northerners and their supporters. Here Confederate scouts seldom operated. Major General Patton Anderson, commanding the District of Florida, acknowledged his inability to observe Union movements on the east bank. When the enemy withdrew four regiments from Palatka and carried them across to Picolata, Anderson did not know if they had marched to St. Augustine to be shipped north, or marched down the east bank to Jacksonville.

He commented that the parallelogram bounded by St. Augustine, Picolata, Jacksonville, and the mouth of the St. Johns River was "wholly within the enemy's possession and . . . it was impossible to keep ourselves well advised of all his movements on that side of the river."[31]

The Federal river patrols created a Union enclave on the east bank of the St. Johns River centered around St. Augustine. Two quotes from contemporary sources demonstrate the success of the inner blockade. In May 1864 John C. Gray, Jr., a Federal officer, stated that "the people on the east side of the St. Johns are called Florida Yankees and the majority of them are Union men."[32] Two months later Lake City's *Columbian* voiced the same sentiments in an editorial praising Captain Dickison while wishing that he had a larger command so that: "We would soon hear of the evacuation of Lincoln's congressional district in East Florida."[33]

It is clear that after the Union Navy closed the mouth of the St. Johns River, Confederate river traffic reversed. Small steamers began carrying goods from Jacksonville upriver then overland to Indian River or the Mosquito Lagoon to be shipped out to sea. Much of this traffic was halted by the inner blockade, although it is noteworthy that as late as February 1864 the *St. Marys* was captured in Jacksonville, loaded with cotton, preparing to run upriver. However, the inner blockade made a significant impact upon Jacksonville, its port, and all of northeast Florida.

Chapter Nine

THE STEAMBOAT ERA

At the end of the Civil War, Jacksonville had to rebuild both the town and the port. Lumbering, which had been a thriving industry before the war, was the first to revive. The relatively new endeavor of catering to the Northern tourist followed closely behind lumbering. Then, in the 1870s, exporting oranges became a third economic factor in the revival of the port. Lumbering relied upon the schooner; the other two were served by the steamboat, both shallow-water and oceangoing types. Naturally, the shallow-water, or coastal steamer, held sway until the channel at the bar of the St. Johns had been deepened; then the ocean going steamers entered the port. The period from 1865 through the 1890s may be considered the steamboat era for Jacksonville's port.

On 3 March 1865, Congress created the Bureau of Refugees, Freedmen, and Abandoned Lands. The Freedmen's Bureau, as it was called, initially concerned itself with providing provisions, clothing, and food for refugees and freedmen. It also established schools and hospitals. It converted the Magnolia Hotel into a hospital and sent many of its patients and medical supplies upriver aboard the *Darlington*, which had been reacquired by Captain Brock.[1]

Northern lumbering interests returned to Jacksonville and the St. Johns River shortly after the end of the war. Ambrose Hart, a New Yorker, commented at the end of 1866 that Jacksonville was full of Northern men building sawmills and re-establishing logging operations upriver. He entered into a partnership with Samuel B. Thompson, who had a logging camp on Black Creek. Much of the timber acreage was government land purchased at $1.25 per acre. Timber carts, with wheels eight feet in diameter, carried their logs, attached by tackle, beneath the axles. The logs would be carried to the creek bank, dropped, and rolled into the water. Then they would be floated down to a place wide enough for the logs to be joined into rafts, generally about five hundred per raft. When assembled, the rafts would be measured, marked, and sold to a sawmill. The raft, or rafts, then would be towed to the mill by tugs.[2]

Hart and Thompson found the price of food and normal supplies exorbitant along the St. Johns. It was cheaper for them to buy their supplies in New York and ship them to Florida. For example, a comparison between Jacksonville prices and the price Hart and Thompson paid at their landing for New York goods reveals:

	Jacksonville price	their price at landing
barrel of pork	$25.00	$21.00
100 lbs. of hay	2.55	1.60
corn per bushel	1.75	1.41

And Hart noted that the prices in Middleburg, near his camp, were even higher than in Jacksonville.[3]

At the end of the war, the government had a surplus of ships to dispose of at attractive prices. The Revenel and Company, shipping interests in Charleston, teamed up with the Leary-Pease-Greenman partners to purchase some of these vessels to reinstate the Charleston-St. Johns River route. Their first steamer was the City Point, a wooden sidewheeler with a normal draft of seven feet which allowed her to cross the St. Johns Bar with ease.

The *City Point* made its appearance on the St. Johns on 23 or 24 November 1865. She was, up to that time, the largest vessel in commercial service on the St. Johns. It took just twenty-four hours from Charleston, and about seventeen from Savannah. Her owners advertised her as offering "a first class table and clean comfortable staterooms at no extra charge."[4]

The winter tourist trade was good enough for the owners to put a second steamer on this route. On 22 March 1866, the *Dictator* arrived in Jacksonville to work with the *City Point*. Captain Louis Mitchell Coxetter was master of the *Dictator*. Coxetter had sailed the Charleston-St. Johns run during the 1850s; his wartime exploits have already been noted.

At the completion of the winter season, the owners sent the *City Point* to New York for repairs and upkeep before joining the New York summer excursion trade. Meanwhile the *Dictator* stayed on the Florida route throughout the lean summer months. This procedure proved advantageous for the owners, and, for several years thereafter, one ship would go north for the summer excursion trade while the other remained on the St. Johns.

The two steamers' winter schedules meshed so that the *City Point* departed Charleston in the evening on Friday and arrived back on the afternoon on Wednesday. The *Dictator* left on Tuesday and returned on Sunday. Palatka was the terminus for the ships. Here the more adventurous could connect with Captain Jacob Brock's *Darlington* to continue on to his Brock House at Enterprise on Lake Monroe.[5]

There was great anticipation among the citizens of Jacksonville in mid-April 1870: General Robert E. Lee was coming up the St. Johns. When the steamboat *Nick King* pulled up to the dock, a large crowd was at hand to see this honored gentleman. When the gangplank was secured, a welcoming committee introduced the local dignitaries to the general. Finally, the committee asked General Lee to go out on the upper deck so that those people still on shore could see him. The *Florida Union* reporter wrote: "Not a word was spoken; not a cheer was uttered, but the very silence of the multitude spoke a deeper feeling that the loudest huzzas could not have expressed."[6]

It was quite appropriate that the famous Southern leader should ride on the *Nick King*, for the little steamboat was the former *St. Marys* which had been so active in the Confederate cause and twice scuttled in attempts to keep her from falling into Union hands.

Captain Brock and other river captains made Jacksonville their northern terminus, and competed with the ocean steamers from Jacksonville to Palatka. Many Jacksonville residents utilized these local vessels for day trips upriver for an outing to Green Cove Springs or other destinations for picnics.[7]

Northern visitors who actively promoted Florida as a place to spend the winter were instrumental in bringing others to the St. Johns. Foremost among these people was Harriet Beecher Stowe, who settled in Mandarin, She wrote glowing reports of the advantages of spending the winter in Florida. Her house included a large porch facing the river. When she and her husband were in Mandarin, many steamboat captains slowed down when passing her place, just to give their passengers an opportunity to see the famous lady.

There is a story that Mrs. Stowe was paid by some of the steamboat owners to sit on the porch of her house so that the vessel's passengers might see her. In the early years, either Mrs. Stowe or her husband, the Reverend Stowe, would sit on the porch receiving the silent adulation from the passing tourists. But in 1878, a large pier, jutting 556 feet out into deep water, was built next door to the Stowe's place. This pier made it possible for the large steamers to dock while its passengers rushed ashore to invade the privacy of the Stowes. This disturbing intrusion influenced the Stowes to give up their winter living along the St. Johns at the conclusion of the 1883–84 winter.[8]

In the 1870s citrus became a large commercial crop along the St. Johns, because the river provided a means of transportation in the days before the railroad. Many of the large orange groves had long wharfs jutting out into the river to provide direct loading of the crop for shipment to the north. The smaller groves relied upon an old renovated steamer, the *Orange Maid*, which would steam up and down the St. Johns, picking up the bulk fruit. On board the *Maid,* packers would process and pack the fruit for transshipment at Jacksonville to large steamers headed north. In the 1880s, this industry "represented a $10,000,000 investment with an annual income of $1,250,000 from a yield of 75,000,000 oranges, selling at $15 per 1,000."[9]

Lumbering, tourists, and citrus expanded during the seventies and eighties, bringing more schooners and steamboats to the St. Johns and to Jacksonville. The DeBary line began operations in 1876, and by 1885 it had thirteen steamers operating. It employed over three hundred people. The Plant Investment Company had four steamers on the river, and smaller lines also worked the St. Johns out of Jacksonville. Supposedly, Jacksonville had a total of seventy-four vessels on regular operations from its port. Thus, the various ships had to resort to public relations devices to set themselves above the others. In 1874 the officers of the *Dictator* began wearing dark blue uniforms in emulation of the New York merchant officers. Later a small brass cannon was placed at the bow to be fired upon arrival and departure of the steamer.[10]

Another appeal to the public was to engage in racing with a competitor. In March 1874, the *Dictator* and the Brock Line steamer *Florence* both left Tocoi wharf headed for Magnolia. The *Florence,* on the inside route, aimed directly for the Magnolia wharf. The *Dictator,* trying to cut its competitor off, crossed the bow of the *Florence* to obtain the preferred position. Unfortunately for both vessels, the captain of the *Dictator* misjudged his distance and the strong wind blew the smaller *Florence* into the larger ship. The damage was slight, but the *Florence* lost its chain box and a water cask, which was carried away when water rushed through the open port gangway.

In December of the same year, the *Dictator* ran aground in the St. Johns. It happened on its run from Jacksonville to Palatka during a dense fog. She was rendered immobile, and her passengers expressed great indignation over the captain's incompetency. When the *Silver Springs,* one of the local river steamers, appeared, the *Dictator's* captain arranged for his passengers to be transferred to the smaller vessel for transportation to Palatka. The *Dictator's* crew then shifted the cargo and waited for the rising tide to free their steamer.[11]

Even before work began on the bar of the St. Johns, ocean-going steamers began to appear in the Jacksonville port. In 1878 the *Western Texas* entered the winter tourist trade. Five years later, the Florida Steamship Company brought the *City of Palatka* to Jacksonville. She was an iron-hulled twin-screw vessel, one of the first of her kind to enter coastwise service. She was two hundred feet long, a little over thirty-four foot beam, and had a hold of almost twelve feet. In February 1885, the *City of Palatka* made a record-breaking run from Charleston to Jacksonville in a little over fifteen hours. In 1886 the Clyde Line established service between New York and Jacksonville. The first Clyde steamer was the *Cherokee,* and when it steamed in on 18 November 1886, it was a day to celebrate. The riverside was jammed with people witnessing the event. The Wilson Battery turned out to fire salvos from its twelve-pounder as the steamer tied up at John Clark's dock at the foot of Newnan Street. The Clyde Line added other steamers over the years, including the *Algonquin,* the *Iroquois,* and the *Comanche.*

Ray's Steam Schooner Line followed, offering regular service to Jacksonville. Then the Ocean Steamship Company with the *Kansas City,* the *City of Birmingham,* and the *Le Grande Duchesse* joined its competitors in coming to the St. Johns. The Mallory Line did not operate south of Brunswick, Georgia, until after the St. Johns jetty work was complete. Then it merged with the Clyde Line, forming the Clyde-Mallory Line.[12]

Most of the steamers on the St. Johns in the 1880s were of the eastern sidewheel type, but in 1882 the first of the western steamers arrived. The genus of the western steamers may be traced to Captain Henry M. Shreve's *George Washington,* built in 1816. Fulton's steamer, and the eastern steamboats, followed the tide-water design of having comparatively deep-draft hulls. Shreve, who had gained his initial experience on flatboats on the Ohio and Mississippi rivers, envisioned his hull as a buoyancy chamber, not as a place for the engines and cargo. Thus, his steamer basically was a flatboat with the engine and cargo space on the first deck. [13]

The *Fannie Dugan*, one of the earliest western steamers to ply the St. Johns, was a sidewheeler that began her operations in Portsmouth, Ohio. Her trip from New Orleans to Jacksonville was rough enough to peel paint and smash planking during the heavy seas. When she arrived in port, she was in need of an overhaul and refurbishing inside and out. It took most of August to prepare her for trade on the St. Johns. She only drew thirty-two inches of water when light. Her thirty staterooms, each with two berths, were arranged around her 120-foot salon. Each stateroom had two exits, one into the salon, and the other outside to the rail. On 29 August 1882, she made her first commercial trip upriver to Sanford and Enterprise.

In early October, the *Fannie Dugan* collided with the *Frederick DeBary* near Buffalo Bluff. Both captains claimed that they did all in their power to avoid the mishap, and that the other was at fault. The damage was limited principally to the reputations of the respective captains. The *Dugan's* claim was only twenty-five dollars, for the staving in of one of the paddleboxes. [14]

The *Jennie Lane*, another western steamboat, soon worked in tandem with the *Dugan*, because the two ships had either the same owners or a good working relationship because both were western boats. At any rate, by the end of the year the *Dugan* sailed from Jacksonville to Enterprise on Monday, Wednesday, and Friday. The *Lane* sailed on Tuesday and Saturday. Both arranged their departures from Sanford to take place after the Orlando train had arrived.

Competition became intense on the Jacksonville upriver run. The Baya Line brought in the new sidewheeler *H. T. Baya*, and the DeBary Line added the *City of Jacksonville*. In addition, the *H. B. Plant*, the *Frederick DeBary*, the *Welaka*, the *George M. Bird*, and the *Rosa* ran upriver to Sanford. All of these were competing with the *Flora*, the *Eliza Hancox*, the *John Sylvester*, the

Magnolia, and the *Palatka* from Jacksonville to Palatka. In January 1883, the *Dugan* cut its rates: $3.50 cabin fare to Sanford, $5.00 for meals and stateroom, and $8.00 for a round trip with meals and stateroom. The *Jennie Lane* reduced its rates to the same prices a few days later.

Throughout January the *Fannie Dugan* did well with the lower fares. Unfortunately for the steamer, near the end of the month, while returning from Enterprise, one of her guy wires for the smokestack became entangled in a tree, which caused the stack to collapse, resulting in quite a bit of damage. The crew jury-rigged the stack to allow her to continue on to Jacksonville for repairs. Although the *Dugan* continued operating against her competition for most of the year, she was continuously beset by mechanical problems.[15]

The race between the *H. T. Baya* and the *John Sylvester* ranked on the St. Johns with the famous steamboat races on the Mississippi River. The *Sylvester* was built in 1866. She was a wooden sidewheeler, 193 feet long, 30 foot beam, and had a hold of 9½ feet. The *Baya* was a wooden sidewheel vessel built in 1882, 205 feet long, 32 foot beam, and had a hold of 9 feet. The *Baya* was newer, longer, and had more horsepower than the *Sylvester,* yet the latter had a reputation as a fast vessel and was more "finely tuned."[16] A lengthy article in the Jacksonville *Florida Union* by an unknown reporter provides the best source for the race in its entirety.

News of the impending race brought large crowds to the Jacksonville piers. "The two racers of the river started out fresh, graceful and buoyant, nose to nose, each confident . . . cheer after cheer rent the air as the two steamers reached Grassy Point with no change in their relative positions." Some time after that, the *H. T. Baya* gained slightly on its opponent so that, although their sterns were side by side, the bow of the longer *Baya* jutted out in the lead. In this position the two ships rounded the turn in the St. Johns and were lost to the view of the crowd in Jacksonville.

The *Baya* inched forward until she was a half a length ahead of the *Sylvester.* Then the latter pulled alongside, and Captain John

Post and his crew shift the chain box and all of the passengers to the port side, which elevated his steamer's starboard guard above the *Baya*'s. Then closing over the *Baya*'s guards, Post had the passengers and chains moved amidships, dropping his guard down upon the *Baya*. The reporter wrote: "in this familiar fashion the twain proceeded as bosom friends with locked arms to the buoy at Green Cove Springs, turned sharply there and headed for the dock with not one ray of daylight showing between their sides and their passengers shaking hands across the guards of the rival-welded steamers." In addition to the damage done to the guards of the *Baya*, the galley, stove, and dishes were smashed, ending any prospect of meals for the *Baya* passengers on this trip.

The writer continued: "This was the most exciting part of this most exciting race. If the boats had kept their straight course, as it appeared they would do, they would have knocked the dock and the people into the river. Each boat was trying desperately for advantage here. The *Baya* on the right hoped to crowd the *Sylvester* off to the left of the dock and take possession. The *Sylvester*, however, threw her guards above the *Baya*, gave her rudder a sudden turn to starboard, and threw the *Baya* off the dock to shoreward, and the *Sylvester* thus took the dock."

Outmaneuvered, Captain Leo Vogel of the *Baya* outfoxed his opponent by not docking at Green Cove Springs. Instead, he ordered his crew to heave the mailbags ashore while he backed down and headed towards Tocoi. By this action he was a half mile ahead of his rival departing Green Cove Springs. Vogel maintained his lead. He left Tocoi just as Captain John Post brought the *Sylvester* up to the pier.

The *Baya* reached Palatka about five minutes ahead of the *Sylvester*. Unfortunately for Captain Vogel, the *Baya* had not taken on a full supply of coal in Jacksonville, and it was apparent that more would have to be loaded aboard in Palatka. In spite of the urgings of all concerned, the delay to load coal allowed the *Sylvester* to leave ahead of the *Baya*. Vogel's people said they were sixteen minutes behind; Post's crew claimed it was only a six-minute delay.

On the return journey, the *Sylvester* was several miles ahead when it reached Green Cove Springs. Once again, Captain Vogel resorted to the same stratagem of casting the items destined for Green Cove Springs onto the shore without making a landing. Thus he regained the lead, and on the final leg to Jacksonville the *Baya* was about four lengths ahead of its rival.

The reporter wrote that a "half hour before the arrival of the boats, their respective docks were thronged with a pushing, 'scrounging' mass of eager people. When a red light came into sight up the river, a cheer rent the air that was not allowed to subside until the jubilant sky rockets of the *John Sylvester*, this side of Grassy Point, showed the letters H. T. B. on the leading boat. Then the scene that followed baffles description. Shouts and yells and hurrahs, benedictions, congratulations, explanations, vociferations, and every demonstration known to human excitement . . . "

Who really won the race? That question was debated all over Jacksonville. Colonel H. T. Baya was ecstatic over the race and his victory. He claimed that his ship could take the *Sylvester* in a fair race. He noted that his ship was new, the engineers were not familiar with the engine, and the captain was new to the river. He also pointed out that his ship carried a large number of passengers, who at times rushed from one side to the other, causing his ship to list from port to starboard, so that occasionally his captain was dependent upon only one sidewheel for power. Further, he stated that he did not have a chainbox or other heavy object that his crew could shift from side to side to steady his ship to counter the movement of the passengers.

Captain Post claimed victory because he had made all of the stops en route. He said that he only carried thirty pounds of steam throughout the race, and that he could have passed the *Baya* on several occasions if his rival had not cut in on him. Post was emphatic that in a fair race he would win, and he was willing to stake money on it.

The reporter concluded by saying: "The *Sylvester* is perhaps the best handled boat of the two. Captain Post is a perfect master of her movements and knows her like a book. . . . The talk on the streets last night was that Captain Crawford would have handled the *Baya* better on this river than her new captain who is unacquainted completely with its channels. It was said that fully $10,000 was 'up' on the race and most of this was declared 'off' until a more decisive race would take place."[17] However, the *Baya* was too large for the St. Johns River. It could not handle the river bends well enough to remain in Florida service. In a short time she was sent to the New York area to be used in the excursion business.

Besides engaging one another in steamboat races, the river captains encountered a new challenge from nature at about this time. In the late 1880s or early 1890s (sources are vague as to the exact time), people living along the St. Johns River were enthralled by the addition of a beautiful floating water plant to the river's scenery. Above a luxuriant green base towered a spike of purple flowers. Steamboat operators were pleased when the tourists admired the drifting bouquets gliding by their vessels.

The recipient of this attention was the water hyacinth, a freshwater, free-floating plant. From its dark green bulblike leaf base grow bright green upright leaves, which serve as sails in the wind, crowned by a tall spike of purple flowers rising three to four feet in height above the water's surface. Below the surface a bushy mass of fibrous roots extends out six to twenty-four inches. The flowers last only a day or two before they fade. Then the flower stalk bends, thrusting the spent flowers and seed pods under water. When ripened, the pod releases the seeds which settle to the bottom or are entrapped in the mass of roots. The seeds remain fertile for seven or more years.

During warm-weather months along the St. Johns, the seeds may produce two crops in their growing season, with a third ready to mature the next spring. However, most of the plants are reproduced by the vegetative process as stolons develop from the healthy parent plant. In a short time these offspring emit their own stolons, reproducing more individual plants. The proliferation of the water hyacinth borders on the fantastic: it doubles its area every month of its growing season. In Florida, where it has no natural enemies, hyacinth propagation becomes awesome. Here, the plants are killed by floating down to saltwater, or by being exposed to a heavy frost.

W. F. Fuller claimed to have brought this beauty to the St. Johns River, and he believed that "the people of Florida ought to thank me for putting these plants here."[18] Captain W. A. Shaw, of the steamer *City of Jacksonville*, said that Fuller "being a fancier of rare species of plants bought some of the hyacinth seed in New York and planted it in the pond on his place among other lilies that were there growing." True to form, the plants multiplied, and he cast the excess growth into Dunn's Creek.[19] Propagation continued as clumps of water hyacinths drifted about on the St. Johns at the whim of wind, current, and tide, occasionally massing at some bend in the river until the wind shifted. People soon noticed these floating gardens.

By 1893 there were acres of hyacinths floating about until a man-made barrier, the Florida East Coast Railroad bridge at Palatka, impeded the plant's movement downriver. Only in the center, where the draw was, could the hyacinths pass. When a prolonged south wind pushed the floating masses against the bridge, a plant jam occurred. The hyacinth became so entangled, both above and especially below the water, that none of the plants passed, even in the center at the draw. For the first time, the wide St. Johns was covered from bank to bank. The plant was no longer a picturesque floating garden; now it was a menace to navigation, a green menace.

The next year, 1894, when the railroad rebuilt its bridge with the same low braces from piling to piling, the rivermen protested this dangerous design. They called upon bank president E. S. Crill to state their case. Crill wrote to his congressional representative, C. M. Cooper, saying: "If this bridge is constructed so they can pass through they will go out with the tide, and, when they strike salt water, die. . . . it will cost thousands to remedy what can be done now with little or no extra expense."[20] Cooper called upon the Corps of Engineers for aid.

Crill and the Corps were not the only ones concerned by the arrival of the water hyacinth. The Department of Agriculture sent Professor H. J. Webber of Eustus to Jacksonville to investigate the plant. Because of its concern over this threat to river navigation, the Clyde Line entertained the professor as its guest on his trip downriver from Sanford to Jacksonville.[21]

The rivermen were afraid this approach was too passive; they wanted more positive action. J. E. Lucas, owner of three steamboats, represented the boat owners when he made a trip to Washington to see the secretary of war. Lucas carried photographs to substantiate his point. One picture showed his three boats in line near the railroad bridge, struggling to move through the hyacinth mass. He said that "in three hours they were able to get ahead only 100 feet."[22] Another picture portrayed his crews standing on a large plant floe using axes and saws to cut through the entangled mass in order to free his boats.

By January 1897, the *Times-Union* was editorializing about the serious impedance to navigation caused by these pesky plants. In August the summer growth was so great that huge masses of hyacinths flowed downstream past Jacksonville. On one particular morning, the plant jam was thick enough to keep the ferryboat from entering its slip at the foot of Newnan Street. The captain pushed his ship against the hyacinth, then sent two men out on the jam with a hawser to secure the plants. When tied down, he reversed power and hauled the hyacinths out to midstream where "the men unfastened the hawser and stepped aboard the ferryboat, which then re-entered the slip and made fast to the pier."[23]

The next month Captain Beerbower, of the tug *Ida B.*, reported that he had to turn down a number of tows because he did "not know what moment we will have our wheel taken off by some log in the mass of hyacinths." He said that he had already had one wheel broken for that reason and that the *Anne H.* had to replace its shaft because of the plant jam. Later that month visitors were kept from going aboard the gunboat *Nashville* when the plants stopped rowboats from leaving shore. One of the

Nashville's cutters became entangled in a mass and had to drift with the plant flow until extricated by the tide.[24]

The hyacinth growth struck hardest upon the small commercial river boats and recreational boaters, especially in the narrow tributaries where the green menace closed all navigation. In February 1898, the *Ida B.* again had to be hauled up on the ways at the Merrill Stevens yard to replace her shoe and rudder, which had been wrenched off when she tried to force her way through a dense plant jam. The following September, the steamer *Gipsy* took several days to force her way through the hyacinth mass in Haw Creek to Paxton Landing to pick up 190 barrels of naval stores bound for Jacksonville. Paxton Landing had been virtually blockaded by the plants, and there were still several hundred barrels left which the *Gipsy* could not accommodate. Business up the clogged tributaries was coming to a halt, and this was being felt throughout the St. Johns waterway down to the port of Jacksonville.[25]

The Harvesta Chemical Compounding Company of New Orleans contacted the Corps of Engineers to say that it had a spray which could eliminate the hyacinths. In October 1901, the steamer *Le Reve*, a former houseboat rented for private parties, was fitted with a spraying apparatus. When ready, *Le Reve* steamed up the river, dispensing 242,503 gallons of arsenic acid upon Black Creek, Rice Creek, Deep Creek, and Blue Springs, as well as the St. Johns. Not all went well on this voyage. Cattlemen claimed that the solution killed their stock. In 1905 the water hyacinth appropriation in the corps' budget contained a proviso prohibiting spraying in Florida.[26]

From 1906 to 1939 the most effective destroyer of the weeds was the sawboat, which contained a horizontal shaft holding cotton-gin circular saws out in front of the boat. In addition to the forward horizontal axle, there were two other axles mounted as outriggers on each side of the stern of the seventeen-foot boat. After allowing for overlapping, the sawboat destroyed water hyacinth in ten-foot strips as it moved through the mass. The same saws which cut the plants provided propulsion for the boat. Behind the sawboat floated a mass of shredded material which

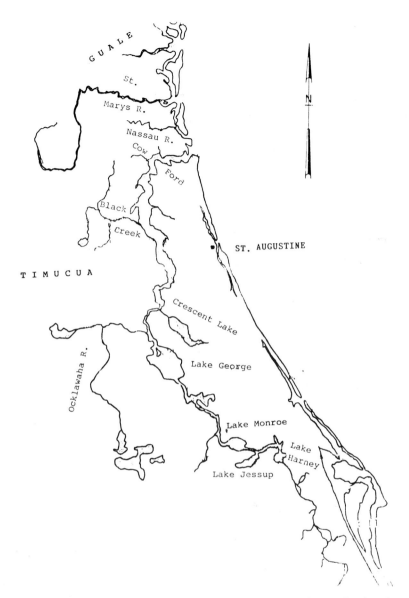

APALACHEE

GUALE

St.

Marys R.

Nassau R.

Cow

Ford

Black

Creek

TIMUCUA

• ST. AUGUSTINE

Crescent Lake

Ocklawaha R.

Lake George

Lake Monroe

Lake
Harney

Lake Jessup

N

Indian Tribes in Florida, 1562

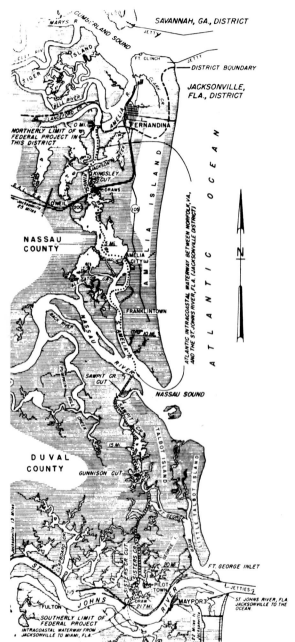

SAVANNAH, GA., DISTRICT

DISTRICT BOUNDARY

JACKSONVILLE,
FLA., DISTRICT

NORTHERLY LIMIT OF
FEDERAL PROJECT IN
THIS DISTRICT

NASSAU
COUNTY

DUVAL
COUNTY

ATLANTIC INTRACOASTAL
WATERWAY BETWEEN
NORFOLK, VA., AND THE
ST. JOHNS RIVER, FLA.
(JACKSONVILLE DISTRICT)

SCALE IN MILES

CORPS OF ENGINEERS
JACKSONVILLE, FLORIDA.

Inland Waterway, St. Marys to St. Johns
Courtesy U.S. Army, Corps of Engineers

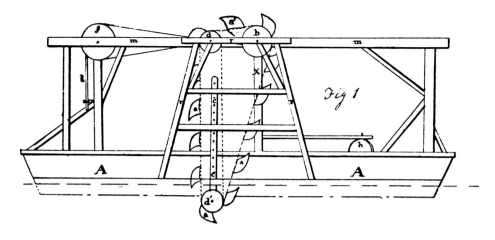

James Grant's Mud Machine
Courtesy National Archives

Union Gunboat at Mayport Mills
Courtesy Florida State Photographic Archives

Steamboats in Water Hyacinths
Courtesy U.S. Army, Corps of Engineers

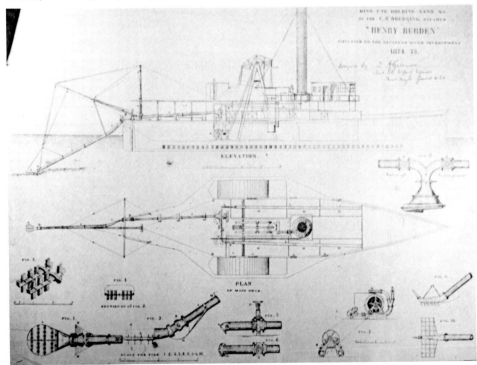

Drawing of *Henry Burden*
Courtesy U.S. Army, Corps of Engineers

Air View of Mouth of the St. Johns River
Courtesy U.S. Army, Corps of Engineers

Blount Island with OPS Crane in Background
Courtesy U.S. Army, Corps of Engineers

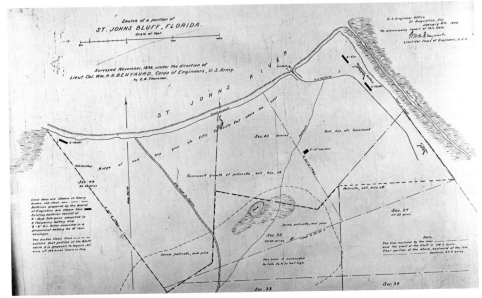

Sketch of St. Johns Bluff Fortifications
Courtesy National Archives

Three Friends Docking the USS *Constitution*
Courtesy *Florida Times-Union*

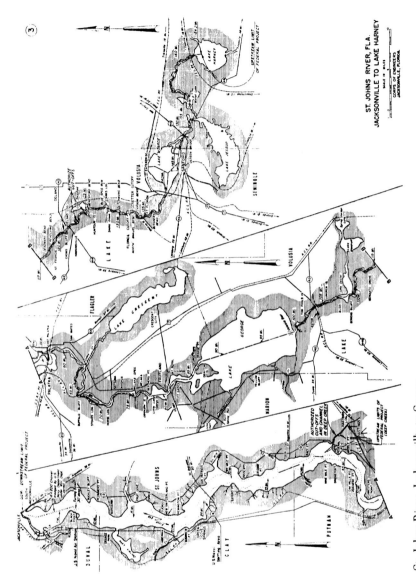

St. Johns River, Jacksonville to Source
Courtesy U.S. Army, Corps of Engineers

U.S. Navy Instructors and Soviet Officers with Lend-Lease YPs at Mayport
Courtesy U.S. Navy, Mayport Naval Station

New Three Tier Loading at TMT
Courtesy Crowley Maritime Corporation

would decompose and sink within two weeks, if it was not carried downstream sooner.[27]

When used properly, the sawboat was 95 percent successful in killing water hyacinths, but the magnitude of the task prevented the United States Hyacinths Destruction Boats from ridding the St. Johns of the green menace. It was considered more effective in areas of great congestion to have the sawboats cut out large patches from the main plant-jams so that the hyacinths might drift downstream to the sea and extinction. In 1932, for example, 1,617,427 square yards of hyacinth jams in the St. Johns were removed by drifting.[28]

The water hyacinth's greatest impact was upon pleasure craft and smaller commercial boats, such as the *Ida B.* and the *Gipsy,* who used the tributary streams. These waterways were periodically blockaded by the hyacinth bloom. The river's tourist trade was not affected, because much of this steaming took place in larger ships, in the winter months, and in channels opened by the sawboats. Thus the hyacinth's impact upon the tourist trade was not great.

But the tourist industry, the mainstay of the steamer traffic into Jacksonville, had already peaked and had entered its decline, as the following figures indicate:

Year	Number of tourists to Jacksonville
1870	14,000
1875	50,000
1885	60,000
1886	65,193
1887	58,460

The peak year was 1886, and the decline the following year was attributed to the active advertising employed by California to sell its climate in competition with Florida.[29] Still, what might be overlooked is the fact that by the 1890s the railroads were making serious inroads into steamer travel. The heyday of the tourist steamers to the port of Jacksonville was coming to an end.

Chapter Ten

DOWN TO THE SEA

In 1867 Dr. Baldwin joined the newly formed Jacksonville Board of Trade. The following year he headed the board's Bar Improvements Committee, and, in that capacity, he was back in Washington seeking funds from Congress.[1] His plea resulted in General Quincy Adams Gillmore ordering several more surveys during 1868 and 1869. The results of these surveys were no different than earlier reports submitted by the Corps in rejecting Baldwin's views. But Jacksonville's drive to the sea could only be delayed; it could not be stopped.

Colonel William Ludlow, in charge of the latest investigations of the St. Johns, wrote Baldwin that Gillmore had discussed many plans with him. They had considered straightening the river channel above the bar to increase the scouring action; constructing piers for the same reason; following Dr. Baldwin's plan of closing Fort George Inlet; and, finally, raking or dredging the bar itself. This last procedure was most agreeable to Gillmore.[2]

After more thought, General Gillmore submitted his plan to rake the bar during the ebb current, when the sand in suspension would be forced out to sea. He also said that Charles H. Campbell had offered to rake and keep the depth at fifteen feet for ten thousand dollars per year. The Corps accepted his proposals.[3]

88

Dr. Baldwin would have worn a smug smile of satisfaction if he had read Gillmore's follow-up report on the dredging operations. The contract was canceled on 22 May 1871, because of lack of success.[4] In fact, Campbell's failure was so complete that Gillmore made no payment for his efforts.

General Gillmore was at the end of his resources. He had no confidence in the practicality of jetties, he did not accept Dr. Baldwin's proposal, and his own scheme of raking or dredging had failed. He was running out of ideas, while Baldwin still exerted pressure on the Corps to do something. This was when Colonel Ludlow provided him with a new and revolutionary answer to his problem: a hydraulic hopper dredge.

Earlier, Gillmore had Ludlow examine the Charleston, South Carolina, harbor. Ludlow's detailed report in April 1871, quoted from a letter to the Commissioners of the State of South Carolina, on 10 November 1857, discussing the improvement to the harbor through the use of a hydraulic hopper dredge, the *General Moultrie*.[5] Gillmore read Captain George W. Cullum's reports of the world's first hydraulic hopper dredge, and he decided to adopt the same method.

The steamer *Henry Burden*, a sidewheeler built to carry passengers, was chartered. She was 132 feet long, 24½ foot on the beam, and drew 5½ feet. She could carry 100 tons on a 7-foot draft. She was a strongly built ship, and, although her deep draft and small carrying capacity hindered her work as a dredge, she had been the best available for charter. She was equipped with a centrifugal pump, two suction hoses, and a bin to hold the sand brought up from the bottom. The *Burden* became the second hydraulic hopper dredge in the United States.

Gillmore made the suction pipe flexible by including a section composed of a six-inch rubber hose covering a spiral spring so that it could ride on the bottom, regardless of the pitching of the *Burden*. He put a two-hundred-pound iron frame on the dredge end of the pipe to weight it down. Below this, at the mouth of the pipe, he fastened metal teeth to stir up the sand and muck. The entire pipe was fifty feet long. Two years later she was modified by replacing her two six-inch pipes with one nine-inch suction pipe over the stern.[6]

The *Henry Burden* would travel outside the bar with its suction pipes raised. Then it would turn, lower the pipes, and steam in slowly to the bar. As soon as it reached the outer edge of the bar, the pumps would be turned on, the ship's speed reduced to barely maintain steerageway, and the *Burden* would cross the bar, sucking up sand and water. Once over the bar, the pumps would be stopped, the pipes raised, and the dredge turned to begin its outward-bound run. The process of lowering the suction pipes, reducing speed, and dredging the bar would be repeated on the outgoing track. These two runs would be sufficient to fill the *Burden's* storage bins. During the outer turnaround, the side gates to the bins were opened, the pipes raised off bottom, the pump run at full speed drawing in clear water, and the storage areas flushed out. It took the *Burden* six minutes to turn at the completion of each run. Very little time was lost during these dredging operations.[7]

In the early years of the 1870s, the old sidewheeler might be seen at the mouth of the river, chasing the elusive channel, while it brought up the sand and muck. The winter of 1871–72, the *Burden* removed almost forty-eight thousand cubic yards, cutting a channel fifteen feet deep at high tide. But the storms which lashed the mouth of the St. Johns during the winter of 1873–74 deposited more sand than she could handle. Each time the channel was dredged, another storm would fill it up.

Gillmore became discouraged. He wrote: "The natural and proper port for the shipment of all freight arriving in east Florida, is Fernandina, and the inside passage should be enlarged. . . . I doubt the wisdom of expending any more money upon the bar at the mouth of the St. Johns River."[8] When the appropriations ran out, Gillmore retired the *Henry Burden* from service on the St. Johns, and soon the water over the bar was a mere six feet.

The St. Johns River bar was a hindrance to the economic growth of the whole region. Not only did the shallow bar keep out, or delay, deep draft vessels from using the port of Jacksonville, but the sinuous channel caused groundings and shipwrecks which drew scavengers to the river's mouth. From 1850 to 1868, excluding the war years, there were five sailing ships and two steamers lost while attempting to cross the bar.[9] In addition to those seven major disasters, there were innumerable minor mishaps due to piloting errors.

When the brigs *Neva* and *John* grounded after missing the channel, their cargoes were rifled by crewmen of ships inside the bar and by the local residents living ashore. The New York Board of Underwriters increased its insurance rates for the port because of these events. The Jacksonville Board of Trade tried to explain that things had changed along the mouth of the St. Johns, that the undesirable elements had moved, to be replaced by "owners of the soil, honest, and industrious," but to no effect; the insurance rate increase remained.[10]

Standing off, waiting for deep water, was a frequent occurrence harmful to trade. Conditions worsened after the *Henry Burden* left the St. Johns River. At one time in 1874, twenty-two ships were locked inside the bar waiting for deep enough waters to leave port. One of those ships had been waiting more than six weeks.[11] Almost a decade later, in January 1883, more than a dozen ships were waiting to escape Jacksonville. Most were three-masted schooners carrying yellow pine to the north. Captain Somers Hand of the *Ridgewood* left Jacksonville on 20 December 1882, and on 8 January 1883, he still was at Mayport waiting for high water. He grumbled that he had traveled twenty miles in nineteen days.[12] Jacksonville's business community suffered, but not in silence.

Back in 1878, Dr. Baldwin had raised money to bring Captain James B. Eads to Jacksonville. Eads, an authority on hydraulic engineering, who had gained fame for his daring jetty work at the mouth of the Mississippi, studied the local situation. He recommended that two converging jetties be built to create a stable twenty-foot-deep channel out to sea. The price was high, an estimated $1.7 million. Still, Captain Eads felt it was a small cost to open Jacksonville up to the world, and influential Jacksonvillians agreed. Congress was besieged with pleas from the city.[13]

Again, General Gillmore, in New York City, felt the pressure. He sent Assistant Engineer George Daubeney to the St. Johns for yet another survey. Daubeney came up with a plan similar to Eads's suggestion. Gillmore, accepting his proposal, drew up plans for permanently fixing and deepening the treacherous, elusive channel. Gillmore favored low or submerged jetties rather than the high ones proposed by Eads. Of the two, the northern one was to be ninety-four hundred feet, while the southern one would be sixty-eight hundred feet in length. Gillmore felt that if all the river's waters were trapped and channeled through the jetties, the force of the current would be too great, resulting in excessive scouring of the river bed. He designed his jetties so that from the shore out they would be submerged, with the last two thousand feet being built up to one-half tide level. The early sections being submerged would allow the ebb flow waters rushing out to spill over the jetties, reducing both the velocity and volume of water contained to scour the cut. Gillmore assumed his method would result in a channel fifteen feet deep at mean low water. Congress adopted his plan on 30 June 1879, with an appropriation of $125,000.[14]

Lieutenant Walter L. Fisk, the officer in charge of the St. Johns River project, began work on 10 November 1880, at Fort George Island. He awarded his first contract to Lara, Ross, and Company of Wilmington, North Carolina. Roderick G. Ross arrived on the site that month to begin a long career working on the St. Johns River.

Ross's foundation for the stone jetty was a mattress of logs nine inches in diameter at the small end, fastened together, with a top layer of loose brush a foot thick.[15] These rafts were towed out to sea and sunk in place. In March 1881, Fisk let another contract to J. H. Durkee, a Jacksonville firm, to work on the foundations. Midway through the year, the southern jetty had its initial layer, and the first rafts of the northern pier were being placed.[16]

During the building of the foundations, the mouth of the St. Johns was in a cycle of two channels. Ships used the southern route. Fisk left a three-hundred-foot gap open in the south jetty for shipping until the northern channel was scoured and stabilized. Gillmore's plan seemed to be working well. Still, Lt. Fisk and his successors faced a series of unexpected problems which challenged their engineering skills.

In 1885 Ross recounted that a person, claiming to have a patent on that type of foundation, obtained an injunction stopping his work. Ross decided to make his foundation using fascines of brush. It proved successful and the work continued.[17]

Another unexpected happening took place on the south jetty, where some water routed around the south or outer side with enough velocity to scour the sand from under the foundations. Lt. Fisk had to construct several spur jetties perpendicular to the south pier to correct this fault. Then, serious erosion took place on the south jetty, because, at times during the ebb flow, the river water was so much higher than the Atlantic waters that the river flowed over the jetty with enough velocity to carry away part of the bottom sand next to the foundation. Fisk solved this problem by raising the jetty height. But Captain James C. Post, his successor, was confronted with a new problem. The extra weight added to the jetty caused appreciable settling of the foundations. In some places the structure dropped fifteen feet. In one night a section sank six feet.[18] And so it seemed to go for the resident engineers.

The early rock hauled in for the jetties consisted of huge blocks of granite shipped from New York in seagoing barges. Sometimes these carriers would arrive during storms and would have to remain at sea until conditions changed. Even in good weather it required the utmost in seamanship and engineering skills to correctly dump the stone in its proper place. Florida limestone was not as heavy as the New York product, but, when some of it was used, it was found to be superior. The marine life had an affinity for the local stone, growing rapidly over the structure, cementing the blocks together naturally. Eventually, only local limestone was used in the jetty.[19]

To add to the engineers' construction problems, Congress was erratic in appropriating money for the project. The original plan called for $1.7 million, and in 1884 the Jacksonville interests had petitioned for an additional $0.6 million. Both sums were on a grand scale, compared to actual allotments.

1880 Congress granted..........................$125,000
1881 Congress granted..........................$100,000
1882 Congress granted..........................$150,000
1884 Congress granted..........................$150,000
1885 Congress granted..........................$150,000

The result of this piecemeal funding was to have the engineers operate from hand to mouth. Often, while waiting for more money, the scouring actions would do so much damage that a major portion of the next appropriation would be spent repairing damage. By the time the corrections had been made, the project's funds would be low again.

Gillmore wrote in 1883 that: "The work of improving the mouth of the St. Johns River has been for sometime past, and is still, in a critical condition. Ample means should be furnished to proceed with the work, and to protect it thoroughly." Two years later, Captain William T. Rossell stated: "During the progress of the work, from its commencement on 14 December 1880, up to the present time it has been idle, through lack of money, for more than a year. The damage caused by these delays has materially increased the cost of the work." Again, in 1887, Captain Black complained of the dangers of inadequate funding.[20]

The project gradually took shape. Almost 4.5 million cubic yards were scoured out of the channel. Yet when the Corps reviewed the jetty work, it found that Gillmore's submerged piers were not able to produce a fifteen-foot channel as desired. His original plan was revised so that the jetty heights were raised to normal high tide from the shore outward. This produced sufficient scouring to create the fifteen-foot channel.[21]

Jacksonville leaders realized that pinning down and deepening the elusive St. Johns River channel over the shoal ground in the Atlantic was not enough. The river, from the mouth to the city, must be improved. These same men considered this a financial task they must undertake themselves. In 1891 the people passed a bond issue for port improvements, the first for Duval County. The county raised three hundred thousand dollars, which was made available to the federal government to remove shoals and dredge the river bed up to the city. The Corps of Engineers carried out the task using this local funding.[22] By 1895 there was fifteen feet over the bar and an eighteen-foot channel up to the city. Jacksonville had become a seaport twenty-five miles upriver from the Atlantic Ocean.

A seaport, no matter where it is located, must keep up with its rivals, and with the developing maritime technology. Hardly had the harbor improvements been established before the Jacksonville Board of Trade wanted deeper water. Congress set aside $350,000 in 1902 for the construction of a twenty-four-foot channel. The two jetties, the southern two and a half miles long, and the northern three miles long, jutting out into the Atlantic only sixteen hundred feet apart at the outer end, had done their job. Now the dredge must be employed to provide the deeper channel.

The increased current flow due to the bar project and the river dredging caused the river banks in some places to become undercut, sending vast amounts of earth into the river bed. Erosion of the banks at St. Johns Bluff and Dames Point were especially severe. Over a ten-year period, the banks at St. Johns Bluff moved back several hundred feet. Unfortunately for posterity, this erosion caused the site of Jean Ribault's Fort Caroline to slide to the bottom of the St. Johns River. The present Fort Caroline is a replica of the original. Erosion ended with the building of retaining walls and the throwing up of riprap (a sustaining wall of stones put together without any formal order) at various places along the river bank. Chaining the St. Johns Bar had spread construction upriver.[23]

The whole concept of opening Jacksonville to the sea as a viable seaport demanded greater and greater efforts to improve the channel. By 1909 the Board of Trade wanted a thirty-foot channel. Ships were larger; the twenty-four-foot depth was not enough. According to business sources of the time, foreign ships could load comfortably to twenty-seven feet. Therefore, many lines stopped off at nearby deep water ports to discharge part of their cargo to lighten ship for a visit to Jacksonville. Business interests worried that shippers might bypass Jacksonville altogether. It seemed as if the region always was a bit behind in its efforts to be a first-class port.

During the thirty-foot-depth work phase, several dredges were employed, not without mishaps. On 5 August 1912, the St. Johns led the second dredge, the Key West, out of the river to empty their dredge bins into the Atlantic. As Captain J. A. McKee passed the mouth of the jetties, the St. Johns's steering gear failed, and the current swung her southward into shoal water, where she grounded. The next morning, the tugs Three Friends, Volunteer, Martha Helen, and Biscayne gathered about the dredge to pull her off, but their combined efforts failed.

On the third day, Captain McKee and his crew had to abandon the St. Johns because she was hogged (a term meaning the opposite of sagging; thus, the ends of the ship drooped lower than the midship section. This causes the keel and bottom to strain and curve upward.), her seams had opened some fifteen feet, and the seas were increasing. By the fourth day, the dredge was disintegrating hourly under the pounding of the sea, and the saga ended.

The St. Johns's graveyard was off the extreme end of the south jetty, to the east of the place where the Dutch steamship Zeeburg had been wrecked. The dredge's location was opposite the spot where the steamship Chatham had gone down off the north jetty. The Chatham, of the Merchants and Miners Line, had been dynamited earlier as a navigational hazard. These three ships, all steel hulls and steam powered, had been lost off the mouth of the jetties during a three-year span.[24]

The Atlantic, an 800-ton, 150-foot long, 30-foot-beam private dredge, owned by the Standard American Company of Oakland, California, also worked on this project. On 31 August 1916, water flowed into her hull from an opening caused by cable chafing, and she sank in the St. Johns River in 34 feet of water. The company brought its divers from Los Angeles, New York, and New Orleans to Jacksonville for salvage operations. The three divers sealed up the hull. Then air was pumped into the hull while water was withdrawn to allow the internal pressure to remain steady. Gradually the *Atlantic* floated to the surface. Most experts agreed that this novel approach saved thousands of dollars over the older method of using derricks. Still, throughout the salvage operations the derrick from Merrill Stevens Shipyard stood by, just in case.[25]

Even routine maintenance could be hazardous. On 17 September 1928, the pipeline dredge *Welaka*, dredging and dumping the material around the north jetty, was lashed by a northeaster. For several days the *Welaka* bounced and bobbed in the rough waters, damaging three or four of its pipeline sections.

Jacksonville's port came into its own during World War II. The Main Street Bridge was completed just before the war, ending the ferry service across the river. But the withdrawal of the ferry boats was little noticed, with all of the other activities taking place. Shipyards on both sides of the river expanded to meet wartime demands. From Main Street to Commodore Point was a hive of activity. Liberty ships and small vessels were built in Jacksonville and extensive repairs were made to ships already in service.

During this time the Corps completed new studies on the channel and recommended construction of a cutoff from Fulton to Dames Point. This would eliminate 1.9 miles of travel, but, more importantly, it would bypass some rather difficult bends in the St. Johns channel, and its proposal was adopted.

The Fulton Cutoff benefited from modern technology. Unlike the earlier years when, as jetties were built, one improvement led to another major disturbance, the Fulton Cutoff was studied first on a scale model by the U.S. Waterway Experiment Station of Vicksburg, Mississippi. Most of the problems were ironed out before actual construction. Work began on 10 July 1950, and the final cleanup blasting was over by January 1952, giving Jacksonville a shorter, deeper exit to the sea.

The Fulton Cutoff created a large island in the St. Johns River, first known as Goat Island and later named Blount Island. It became a major industrial site for the city, offering excellent waterfront facilities for oceangoing vessels. By this time, the Jacksonville Port Authority was the city's agency responsible for harbor improvement. The Port Authority traces its lineage through the Jacksonville Chamber of Commerce back to the early Board of Trade, of which Dr. Baldwin was one of the prime movers.

In 1951, when Ribault Bay became the Mayport Naval Station, the navy dredged out the carrier basin, and also deepened the bar channel to forty-two feet to accommodate the giant aircraft carriers. And these mammoth aircraft carriers were but precursors of the monstrous commercial vessels being built for world trade. In October 1965 Congress authorized a thirty-eight–foot depth from the Atlantic to mile twenty, just below the Jacksonville Port Authority's Tallyrand Avenue docks. Building a viable port is a never-ending task.[26]

Chapter Eleven

FILIBUSTERING

The port of Jacksonville played an important role in sustaining the Cuban Revolution, and in creating sympathies for its cause among Americans prior to the outbreak of the Spanish-American War. Filibusterers brought volunteers, supplies, and munitions to Cuba to aid the rebels in their fight against the Spanish Colonial forces. A cadre of news reporters in Jacksonville supplied the American press with stories of the filibusterers and the rebels, which helped establish the rebel cause as the one deserving of American respect and support.

José Alejandro Huau, born in Cuba of an American father and a Cuban mother, was the linchpin of the filibustering activities of the Jacksonville port. Huau spent five years visiting in the United States early in his life, prior to being expelled from Cuba in 1869 for his part in the Cuban Revolution, known as the Ten-Year War. He moved to Jacksonville in 1870, established a successful tobacco factory and store, and five years later became a naturalized citizen. In the 1880s, he entered local politics, serving three two-year terms as a city councilman. His friendship with Napoleon B. Broward, later governor of Florida, John M. Barrs, a prominent Jacksonville attorney, and George A. De-Cottes, a fellow councilman and important businessman of the city, aided Huau after he became involved in the Cuban

Revolution in the 1890s. Working with him for the cause was his nephew and active collaborator, Alfonso W. Fritot.

Undoubtedly it was through Huau's efforts that José Martí, founder of the Cuban Revolutionary Party who later became the national martyr to its cause, visited the city on eight occasions. The rear of Huau's cigar store was the meeting place for Cubans and their sympathizers during the filibustering years before the Spanish-American War. In fact, visitors to the store represent a listing of participants in the Cuban Revolutionary Movement, from Cuban patriots to filibusterers to newsmen. Besides Martí, General Emilio Núñez, head of the Department of Expeditions; General Enrique Collazo, an active military commander; Gonzalo de Quesada, secretary; and Benjamin Guerra, treasurer, of the Revolutionary Party, all made plans for the revolution in Huau's store. The two Broward brothers, Napoleon and Montcalm, who, along with George DeCottes, owned the seagoing tug *Three Friends*, W. A. Bisbee, owner of the *Dauntless*, and "Dynamite Johnny" O'Brien, at one time captain of both ships, met there to plan gunrunning. Among the newspaper correspondents were Ralph D. Paine, Ernest W. McCready, Stephen Crane, and possibly Sylvester Scovell.[1]

Huau's store was one of the major Cuban revolutionary centers in Florida. Huau organized his first venture on 18 January 1895, when he employed three ships to sail from Fernandina to Cuba carrying Martí, a detachment of soldiers, eight hundred rifles, and thousands of rounds of ammunition. A U.S. Treasury agent discovered the plot in time to prevent the ships from leaving port. It then took all of Huau's political and social skills to convince Colonel James B. Anderson, inspector general of Florida's state troops, not to confiscate the rifles and ammunition seized.[2]

Huau's business prospered, allowing him to devote much time to his revolutionary efforts. He worked closely with Alfonso Fritot, who was the agent for all railroads running into Jacksonville. Fritot had the authority to route boxcars almost at will, and he even secured special trains or private cars when needed. His services were crucial to Huau's plans. Between the two men, expe-

ditions were organized, boats chartered, and supplies shipped for
the Cuban cause.

Of course, the Spanish knew what these men were doing and
had their homes and businesses under constant surveillance. The
Spanish vice-consul in Jacksonville had specific orders to keep
the two under close scrutiny. Sometimes there were as many as
nineteen Pinkerton detectives at a time watching and reporting
on Huau's and Fritot's movements.[3]

Early in 1896 the U.S. Cutter McLane found a filibusterer in
the Gulf of Mexico and forced it into Tampa. Its cargo was
marked groceries and consigned to John G. Christopher, a Jacksonville merchant and Cuban sympathizer. The Tampa inspectors had no authority to search the cargo, and so they released it
to go by rail to Jacksonville. When Fritot received the freight, he
had it off-loaded at night in a warehouse at the foot of Newnan
Street. Huau then chartered Napoleon Broward's tugboat the
Three Friends to carry General Enrique Collazo, with a company
of soldiers, and to meet and then tow the schooner Stephen R.
Mallory, loaded with supplies, to Cuba.

On 11 March Broward made preparations for his trip to Cuba.
Early in the morning, with no attempt to hide his actions, he
loaded a naphtha launch and two yawls on deck. Then Broward
cast off to head down river to the warehouse dock where his cargo
was waiting. This short trip took Broward past the cutter Boutwell. After stowing the cargo, he steamed down river to George
DeCottes's mill, where he picked up General Collazo and his
troops. Then Broward got up steam and headed out to sea at high
speed. The next morning he was fifty miles southeast of the St.
Johns Bar at the helm of a freshly painted white tug named The
Ox, instead of his steel-gray tug the Three Friends, headed for the
lighthouse at Cardenas on Key Pedro.

Broward's Cuban pilot missed his mark by a few miles, but the
off-loading began anyway. Halfway through the operation, a
Spanish gunboat loomed up out of the darkness. Broward waited
anxiously for his crew to return from shore, and, as soon as they
were aboard, he headed east along the Cuban coast. He ordered

fat pine stuffed in the furnace to make dense black smoke roll out of the stack. The Spanish captain thought that Broward was trying to double back to his landing and he turned back. Broward outfoxed the Spaniard and headed north. On Sunday, 22 March, Broward steamed into the St. Johns in his white tugboat under its proper name, and with half of his cargo still in the ship's hold. Many people guessed at what had happened, but no proof was forthcoming.[4]

As the Cuban Revolution progressed, newspaper editors found reader interest in the struggle to the south. The major papers began to compete for lurid headlines of the war. For correspondents the best source for articles was with the rebels in the interior of Cuba. The problem was how to get there. One could take a steamer to Havana, cross the Spanish military lines, and look for a rebel band to join up with. Of course, the Spanish government tried to keep newsmen from leaving their territorial control. If one did succeed, there was still the problem of finding a rebel band. Most newsmen could not speak Spanish, and while wandering around the countryside looking for revolutionaries they would be liable to be shot by Spanish soldiers, or robbed by bands of peasants for their money, clothes, or well-made American boots. Or one could join a filibustering expedition and be taken into the interior by junta representatives. Many newsmen came to Florida to try this latter route.

Joining a filibustering expedition also had its perils. First, there was the danger of being arrested by the U.S. government as it tried to maintain its neutrality. If caught, one faced arrest, fine, and imprisonment. If successful in reaching Cuba, one still faced the prospect of being captured or killed by Spanish authorities. On 28 April 1896, Ona Melton, a reporter for the Jacksonville *Times-Union*, along with the crew of the schooner *Competitor*, was captured off the Cuban coast. Although he and several others claimed to be Americans, the Spanish military court handed down the death sentence for all. Melton's sentence caused a sensation in the American press. Eventually, the Spanish relented and released all seven men in November 1897, a year and a half later.[5]

Two months after Melton's capture, a shipment of arms and ammunition from Tampa arrived in Jacksonville for the Cuban junta. At the same time, rumor spread that Broward planned a second expedition to Cuba. The government ordered the cutter *Boutwell* back to Jacksonville from Savannah to keep an eye on the *Three Friends*. About the same time, people living on Fort George Island and at Mayport reported a large steamer off the St. Johns Bar. At first some thought that it was a Spanish warship, but it turned out to be the *Laurada* from New London, Connecticut. She was another filibusterer waiting for the *Three Friends*. Captain Broward played his role as a working tug owner to the end. He even invited Captain W. F. Kilgore of the *Boutwell* to join him in his journey to Key West, his purported destination.

On 21 May the collector of customs received orders from the secretary of the treasury to hold the *Three Friends* in port. Kilgore moved his cutter up and trained his guns upon the tug. At dawn Broward cast off and headed down to "Woodlawn," Alexander Merrill's estate, with Kilgore in his wake. Merrill, part owner of Merrill-Stevens Engineering Company, used his steam launch *Lillian* to transfer cargo from shore to the tug anchored in midstream. When the loading was completed, Broward turned and headed back to Jacksonville with Kilgore right behind him.

When Broward found out about Washington's orders, he invited the collector of customs to board him and inspect the cargo. The collector found all of Broward's crates marked "ship stores." When he reported this to his superiors, there was nothing to do but free the *Three Friends*. Broward left the next night, crossing the St. Johns Bar with the cutter trailing him. However, in the darkness, Broward eluded the cutter, and he was free to get on with his journey. Meanwhile, a special train filled with Cuban patriots left Tampa for Panama Park, just north of Jacksonville, where the Cubans debarked, boarded a small boat, and steamed down the river to the *Kate Spencer*. The *Spencer* carried some to the *Laurada* and landed others on the sand dunes south of Pablo Beach (later renamed Jacksonville Beach) where Broward's boats picked them up.[6] On 3 June Broward brought his tug back to Jacksonville without letting anyone know where he had been.

A week later the Jacksonville paper reprinted an article from a northern paper that arms and ammunitions had been landed at a deserted point near Punta Gorda, Cuba. It went on to say that the *Three Friends* planned to reload and return to Cuba, this time with Colonels Leyte, Núñez, and Artego aboard. The *New York Times* reported that the *Record* of Philadelphia had information that one of the largest filibustering endeavors yet undertaken was about to begin. The *Three Friends* from Jacksonville would carry General [Jacksonville sources called him Colonel] Francisco Leyte Vidal, recruits, and munitions; the *Commodore*, from Charleston, would have Colonel Emilio Núñez as its Cuban commander; and the schooner *Stanbury*, from Port Tampa, would carry additional supplies for the rebels. "Fearing the fate of her consort, the *Competitor*, the *Stanbury* will approach the coast of Cuba where things are less warlike, leaving the western end of the islands to steamer vessels."[7] Of course, Broward denied all of this. Yet on 17 June Colonel Leyte did arrive in Jacksonville and boarded Broward's tug for a trip downriver to Woodlawn.

When the Spanish consul heard about this, he chartered a small boat to check up on Leyte's actions. Upon rounding a bend in the river, he came upon the *Three Friends* openly loading crates and several small surfboats aboard. The consul returned to Jacksonville to find authorities to stop Leyte. It was after dark before he located the marshal and the collector of customs and made his charges. He swore Broward was loading an expedition for Cuba. He insisted that time was essential, for once the tug was loaded it would leave immediately and be beyond their jurisdiction. The three hurried to the wharf only to find that, because the consul had not paid a deposit on the boat, it had been rented to someone else. More time was consumed before they located another boat and headed downriver. By now it was almost three in the morning. As they hurried to the illegal rendezvous, they met Broward steaming back to the city; the consul's charges seemed false.

Later that day, Broward did depart Jacksonville. He had a partial load aboard the *Three Friends*. He planned to receive the rest of his cargo from the steamer *City of Key West* somewhere off the keys. The steamer carried sixty Cubans when she left Key West. Later in the day, when the Key West collector of customs learned that the *Three Friends* had left Jacksonville, he sent the Revenue Cutter *Winona* after the steamer.

The next day the captain of the *Winona* stopped the steamer, put aboard a prize crew, and ordered the steamer back to Key West. While returning, the prize crew sighted a small steamer off Alligator Light laying off Knights Key. The Revenue officers observed the steamer launch a small boat, which headed toward them. Then someone on the steamer must have felt that something was wrong, possibly seeing the trailing Revenue Cutter, and recalled its boat. At that the captain of the *Winona* sent an officer over to the steamer, which turned out to be the *Three Friends*, to arrest it and bring it into Key West also. In port a search of the Broward's cargo disclosed only a few boxes of ammunition, which was not considered enough to classify his voyage as an "armed expedition." He was released, sailed to Florida Key where he loaded forty-five Cubans and a cache of ammunition, and continued on to a landing at Juan Clara, on the south coast of Pinar del Rio.[8]

It was 22 June 1896 when Broward landed his passengers and munitions at Juan Clara. Charles Govin, a young correspondent for the Key West *Equator-Democrat* was traveling with the Cuban rebels. Three days later he was captured along with several insurgents. On his way to prison, the officer in charge found out he was an American. The officer bound Govin to a tree and then had him hacked to death with machetes. The New York *World* broke this story on 18 August, and the New York *Journal* carried additional details on 14 September 1896.[9]

After the landing, Broward steamed for Fernandina. When he refused to state the ports he had visited, an official of the State Board of Health quarantined his tug until it could be steam sterilized. Three days later Broward brought the *Three Friends* into Jacksonville, where he received a hero's welcome. The *Times-Union* reported that "Every craft that can whistle, from a naphtha up to a Clyde line, and every mill along the shore from Mayport to the city welcomed the boat." And rising above all the others was the *Three Friends'* whistle "sounding like a Cunarder."[10]

Escorted by the *Dauntless*, the *Kate Spencer*, and the *Martha Helen*, the *Three Friends* steamed up the St. Johns while hundreds of people lined the banks and docks to wave. Huau stood at the dock to lead Broward to the bunting-covered carriage where Mrs. Broward sat waiting. The carriage followed a band which wended its way through the downtown streets to Broward's house in East Jacksonville.[11] It was obvious that the filibusterers were popular heroes, and that American sympathies lay with the Cuban rebels. Newspapers extolled the exploits of these adventurers. Later, in Broward's case, the road to the governor's mansion in Tallahassee was much smoother because of his filibustering days.

In spite of the overwhelming goodwill expressed by the citizens, such public displays limited the usefulness of the *Three Friends*. Not only was Broward's tug under close security, but another well-known filibuster, the *Commodore*, in Charleston, South Carolina, also was being detained. Huau looked about for yet another boat to carry on the war with Spain. In Brunswick, Georgia, the tug *Dauntless* was for sale. She had been built in Camden, New Jersey, was reputed to be among the fastest tugs in the South, and was available for thirty thousand dollars. Huau notified the New York junta of this and an elaborate plan began to develop. Much of the work of deception had to be carried out by Huau and Fritot.

Horatio S. Rubens, the attorney for the New York junta, made a quick and secret trip to Brunswick to buy the *Dauntless*. Then he appeared openly in Jacksonville to hold conversations with Napoleon Broward, giving the impression that the *Three Friends* might be making another expedition to Cuba. At the appropriate time Broward took on a large load of coal and cargo, which alerted all of the surveillance groups. At the same time General Emilio Núñez and Dynamite Johnny O'Brien visited Charleston, playing the same role as Rubens had with respect to the *Commodore*. The Charleston tug also loaded up and appeared ready to go to sea.

In New York, the junta chartered the *Laurada* to take ammunition to Navassa Island, southeast of Cuba, between Haiti and Jamaica. She left Philadelphia on 31 July with papers for Port Antonio, Jamaica. At sea she met three tugs from New York loaded with ammunition and Cuban passengers, which were transferred to the *Laurada*. The steamer headed for Navassa Island immediately.

Meanwhile, thirty Cubans entrained in New York for Charleston, where O'Brien met them and took them to a hotel. The Cubans were followed by about twenty detectives. The next day the Cubans departed in small groups to board a private car of a southbound train, arranged for by Fritot. The detectives had to make do in another car. When the train reached Callahan, Florida, there was a short stop before continuing on to Jacksonville. During that time the last car, the one with the Cubans, quietly was uncoupled, and attached to another locomotive headed to the coast. En route it added two freight cars carrying ammunition. At a bridge across the Satilla River in Georgia, the train stopped to disgorge the Cubans and supplies to be loaded aboard the waiting *Dauntless*. At sunrise on 15 August 1896, the tug headed out to sea on its first filibuster run.

The *Dauntless* was captained by James Floyd, a Jacksonville pilot who had his master's license. O'Brien had high praise for Floyd, although his racist remarks ring strange today. O'Brien stated that: "Floyd was a negro; but everything about him except his skin was white, and he had a great deal of shrewdness."[12] Floyd landed his group at Las Nuevas Grandes, close to Nuevitas Harbor. His eight flat-bottomed skiffs, each propelled by two pairs of oars, guided by a steering oar, scurried back and forth between the tug and shore. After six trips, a searchlight from a Spanish ship was seen in the distance, and Floyd wisely put to sea. At mid-day he was back to complete the debarkation. Then he went to Navassa Island to meet the *Laurada*. The steamer had expected to be met by three tugs, the *Three Friends*, the *Commodore*, and the *Dauntless*. Only Floyd's tug arrived, and so he made two more trips to Cuba, delivering the *Laurada's* supplies to the rebels.

On his way back to Brunswick, Floyd steamed close to Key West, where O'Brien, Núñez, and several others left the tug in a skiff. When Floyd brought the *Dauntless* into port, the collector of customs and the U.S. district attorney questioned his sailors. Six Jamaicans among the crew testified against the others, and the ship was charged with violating the neutrality laws. On 22 September the ship was released under a $7,000 bond and left for Jacksonville.[13]

Filibustering for the Cubans was a never-ending task. While the *Dauntless* was on her mission, Broward was readying the *Three Friends* for another trip, even though the Revenue Cutter *Boutwell* had been ordered to Jacksonville in early August to watch the *Three Friends*, the *Laurada*, and the *Commodore*. On 14 August, Broward loaded aboard four new surfboats, which had been stored at the Florida Yacht Club. Then he steamed down to Mayport; however, the captain of the *Boutwell* ordered Broward to return to Jacksonville to be searched. This was done, and Broward was cleared of any suspicions. Broward made a trip to New York City just to keep his actions as a businessman active. It was 2 September before he announced that he was going to send his tug to Key West, and again he was searched and cleared. This time Broward did not accompany the tug. William Lewis, an experienced tug captain, commanded the *Three Friends*.

Three hours before Lewis departed Jacksonville at midnight, the *Martha Helen* had loaded boxes of arms and departed for sea. At the same time the launch *R. L. Mabey*, docked at the foot of Main Street, took on groups of men dressed as fishermen and left on a "fishing" trip. Once clear of the Revenue Cutter, the three ships rendezvoused in the Atlantic and all cargoes and passengers were put aboard the *Three Friends*. Lewis made a successful landing at Pinar del Rio, off-loading seventy-five Cubans, a small group of American and Russian soldiers of fortune, and a large supply of arms, clothing, and medical equipment. Among the arms was a pneumatic dynamite gun and two thousand pounds of dynamite. On 9 September Lewis returned to Fernandina, where he was quarantined for a week. The Spanish government put much pressure on the American government for action, and finally the *Three Friends* was placed under a $7,000 bond.[14]

On 22 September 1896, when the *Dauntless* finally tied up at her wharf in Jacksonville, Huau had already set in motion plans for her next trip to Cuba. Arms at New York, including the newly invented Sims-Dudley Dynamite gun, were shipped to Jacksonville on a Clyde Line steamer. Meanwhile, Núñez, O'Brien, and other members of the junta had journeyed to Charleston to cast suspicions upon the *Commodore*. Fritot arranged for the private car of the vice-president of the Florida East Coast Railroad to whisk the decoys back to Jacksonville, where two cars of ammunition were attached to the special train. The train then continued south and at New Smyrna two day coaches from Tampa with seventy-five Cubans aboard joined the filibusters. At Palm Beach, passengers and cargo were transferred to the *Dauntless*, which had left Jacksonville on 5 October. The *Dauntless* landed the group at the San Juan River, just east of Cienfuegos, on 13 October. Eight days later, she was laying to off New Smyrna, waiting for a load of coal, when the cruiser *Raleigh* arrested her and took her to Fernandina for quarantine. From then until 29 December she was held by customs in Fernandina and Jacksonville awaiting clearance papers to do salvage work. Captain Kilgore of the *Boutwell* threatened to sink her if she tried to leave without papers.[15]

Early in December 1896, Ralph D. Paine came home to Jacksonville so he could join the filibusterers. He wanted to get to Cuba to write news articles on the revolution. He was a graduate of Yale who had worked on the Philadelphia *Press* for two years. When his managing editor refused his request to be a war correspondent, he called upon William Randolph Hearst for a job. Hearst had a jeweled sword he wanted to send to General Máximo Gómez, and Paine seemed to be the man to take it to him.

Paine came home armed with the sword and went to Huau for information. He was told that if he took a room in the local hotel he would be notified when and where to go.

One night, as he sat on the piazza of the hotel, a Cuban walked by and whispered: "Come to the freight yards at midnight and you will find friends." Right on time Paine arrived at the freight yards loaded down with the sword, two revolvers, and a sheath knife. He found himself among a group of Spanish-speaking men. Soon they began boarding freight cars, and Paine stumbled over someone's leg. The oath he heard was definitely American. Paine had met Ernest W. McCready, a reporter for the New York *Herald*. It was a short run from Jacksonville to Fernandina, where the freight cars were deposited at a wharf alongside the moored *Three Friends*. This time the tug's skipper was Dynamite Johnny O'Brien. [16]

Again Huau and Fritot had employed deception. From all indications it was the *Commodore* that was readying to depart. First the watchman at its wharf had posted signs saying that there was no admittance to the area. Later the captain came out and had the crew move some crossties from the passageway. Earlier two freight cars carrying arms had been moved close to the tug's dock, and, finally, seventy-two Cubans from Tampa arrived. They claimed that they were cigar workers on their way to a factory in Georgia. After dark the Cubans began drifting away, only to assemble at the freight yard for the trip to Fernandina. Meanwhile, the *Three Friends* had slipped out of port with no fanfare, while officials in Jacksonville were watching the *Commodore*.

When newspapers released the story that the *Three Friends* had departed on another filibustering expedition, the U.S. government ordered the *Newark*, the *Raleigh*, the *McLane*, the *Winona*, and the *Forward* to cruise the South Atlantic and the Caribbean for the filibuster.

O'Brien took the tug to the west end of Cuba for his landing. The fog and rain were heavy, just the type of weather for a clandestine debarkation on enemy soil. As O'Brien neared shore, prepared to launch his first boat, the weather lifted a bit, and a

Spanish gunboat saw them. The gunboat closed in, firing its gun at the tug. As he turned north to flee, O'Brien answered with a twelve-pound rapid-fire Hotchkiss gun mounted on the bow of the *Three Friends*. But O'Brien found another Spanish warship to seaward, which joined the chase. O'Brien had a barrel of bacon rinds brought to the stern and burned to release heavy black smoke to hide his escape, and he evaded the warships.

There was no chance to continue the expedition, but at the same time, O'Brien could not return to the United States with his cargo and passengers. He steamed to No Name Key, about forty miles east of Key West, where he off-loaded his illegal party, including the two correspondents. Paine and McCready debated whether or not they could file their stories of the "naval engagement." McCready reasoned that there was no legal problem with their stories because "these newspaper stories of ours will not be accepted as legal evidence, . . . [and] the story will be played up on the front page and it is liable to raise a fuss, but in the eyes of the law all newspapermen are liars until proven to the contrary." Dynamite Johnny O'Brien was proud of his exploit and he looked forward to the publicity. He carried the two stories with him to Key West, where he went for fuel and supplies.[17]

Paine and McCready spent a week on the low sand island with brackish water, rationed food, and a beating sun every day. The junta sent out a schooner with the news that the *Three Friends* could not return to pick them up and it would be a while before another boat could be sent. The two newsmen returned to Key West on the schooner. In port they had mixed news. Their "naval engagement" had made the headlines, and the government was talking of charging those involved with piracy. The good news was that the *Dauntless* had escaped from Jacksonville and was on its way to No Name Key.

Paine and McCready both wanted to complete their trip to Cuba. The problem was: How to get back to No Name Key? They were in luck. Hearst's yacht *Vamoose* was in port and its captain was willing to help Paine get Hearst's sword to General Gómez. As the yacht approached No Name Key, the two correspondents were delighted to see the *Dauntless* being loaded by several small boats. Their delight turned to amazement as the boats scattered like water bugs going every way to hide. When they boarded the tug, they found out that they had been mistaken for a revenue cutter. It took a while to gather up the boats and continue the loading of the expedition. Before they departed, another correspondent joined the group. T. R. Dawley, Jr., had chartered a schooner to find the filibusters. He had been sailing out of Key West, searching for the expedition.

The day of departure was the same day that the *Journal* published Paine's account of the expedition up to his Key West stay. He wrote: "I am writing these last words as the steamer is weighing anchor to head for Cuba. I have been nearly a month en route for Cuba, ten days on the filibuster at sea, with the sea fight as a detail, and more than a week hidden in the swamps of the Florida keys. The *Journal* sword which I am bearing to General Gómez has had a baptism of fire and all sorts of other vicissitudes, but it will reach the commander safely in the end, I am sure."[18]

Unfortunately for Hearst, Paine was not able to keep his word. The commander of this expedition was General Núñez, and his landing was at Pinar del Rio. The general talked Paine out of his mission, telling him that he would be four hundred miles away from Gómez, and it would be impossible for him to travel overland to meet the general. But Paine was assured that there would be expeditions to that portion of Cuba; in fact, the *Commodore* should be leaving Jacksonville at about the time he returned from this expedition.

But the *Commodore* left Jacksonville on the eve of the New Year (that following morning the *Dauntless* was loading the expedition from No Name Key). Stephen Crane was onboard the *Commodore* when she left port. Crane's version of the voyage was published in the 7 January 1897 issue of the New York *Press*. He described how cheerful the Cubans were on loading day. "There was none of that extreme modesty about the proceedings which had marked previous departures of the famous tug, she loaded up as placidly as if she were going to carry oranges to New York instead of Remingtons to Cuba." The tug departed at twilight. On her way downriver she grounded, and the cutter *Boutwell* pulled her off the mudbank. She grounded a second time, but was able to free herself without help.

The groundings may have initiated the problem, but the pounding of the tug by the high seas completed the task. The *Commodore* began leaking about eighteen miles east of Mosquito Inlet. The Cubans manned the pumps, and Crane joined in. Finally, the captain ordered abandoned ship. In Crane's accounting: "Now the whistle of the *Commodore* had been turned loose, and if there ever was a voice of despair and death, it was in the voice of this whistle. It had gained a new tone. It was as if its throat was already choked by the water, and this cry on the sea at night with the wind blowing the spray over the ship, and the waves roaring over the bow, and the swirling white along the decks, was to each of us probably a song of man's end."[19]

Edward Murphy, the captain, saw to the loading of all the Cubans in the two lifeboats. When they had departed, the ten-man crew, plus Crane, were left on board with only a ten-foot dinghy. Murphy ordered Crane, the cook, and the oiler to board the dinghy, and Murphy, who had broken his arm in a fall, joined them. Five others made a raft to brave the storm, and two jumped overboard and drowned. The dinghy was the only craft to survive the seas. Murphy kept the dinghy offshore for thirty hours because of the high breakers on the beach. Then, off Daytona Beach, they risked a landing. The boat capsized, the oiler drowned, and Crane and the other two were cast up on the sand, sole survivors of this filibuster.[20] Crane, who returned to Jacksonville to find another expedition, based his short story "The Open Boat" on this experience.

When the *Dauntless* returned to Jacksonville on 7 January 1897, she was seized by the collector of customs. Two weeks later a $15,000 bond was posted. Then a grand jury examined the crew of the tug, but, by a unanimous vote, the finding was that there was insufficient evidence to indict. When Paine and

McCready had left the *Dauntless*, they had gone into hiding to keep free from the legal proceedings which had been started against the owners of the *Three Friends*. Paine contacted Huau, who supplied him with newspapers to bring him up to date. It included news about the *Commodore* and how their friend Crane had been saved. It also told of the seizure of the *Three Friends* and that a Ralph D. Paine had been accused of piracy. This was because the *Journal* had given Paine a by-line on his article; Mc-Cready, whose article was in the *Herald*, had not received a by-line and was not being sought by the government.

Paine, McCready, and Crane, all still hunting for a trip to Cuba, met and renewed their friendship in Jacksonville. But their days of filibustering were over. The *Herald* ordered Mc-Cready back to New York; the Bacheller Syndicate would not renew its association with Crane, who had lost the gold supplied him when the *Commodore* went down, and Crane too returned to New York; Paine's minister father made arrangements for his son to hide out with an elder of the Presbyterian church in Jacksonville, and Paine turned over Hearst's sword to someone else to be delivered to Cuba. Finally, Paine returned to his work for the Philadelphia *Press*.[21]

Paine related that the sword was eventually given to Huau to deliver. He sent it to the general's wife in Santo Domingo, and she gave it to her husband after the war. General Gómez is supposed to have said: "Ah-h-h, it cost so much money? A trinket good for nothing? Would I be so shameful as to wear it instead of my San[to] Domingo machete? Nonsense! Those imbeciles in New York, with two thousand dollars to waste! It would have bought shoes for my barefooted men, shirts for their naked backs, cartridges for their useless rifles."[22]

After the disaster of the *Commodore*, Huau and the junta decided not to load in Jacksonville for a while. On 17 May 1897, Captain O'Brien headed south with the *Dauntless* to meet the *Alexander Jones* off Palm Beach to pick up cargo for two trips to Cuba. Then O'Brien went to New River Inlet for two carloads of ammunition from the sternwheeler *Biscayne*. Two and a half hours into the loading, the *Marblehead* appeared. O'Brien led the cruiser on a six-hour chase before he was stopped. He was ordered to Key West, where he was inspected. The inspectors reported that everything was in order, and he was released. On 10 June, O'Brien met with the sternwheeler near No Name Key, where he transferred the remainder of the cargo. Then six days later, forty-five miles north-northeast of Key Piedras Light, off Cardenas Harbor, the boiler blew up and he had to resort to sails. Two days later the cutter McLane picked him up off Indian Key and towed him into Key West, where again the crew faced a U.S. commissioner for questioning. Again they were cleared, and their tug towed back to Jacksonville for dry dock and repairs. The cargo was hidden for a later time.

The next expedition took place in mid-October. A two-masted schooner, Silver Heels of Rockland, Maine, was towed six hundred miles down the coast before continuing on under sail for a rendezvous with the Dauntless at Conception Island on the east side of the Bahamas. The tug waited sixteen days before leaving for Key West for coal. The schooner arrived six hours later. The authorities seized the tug, and she was only released on an affidavit stating that she would go directly to Jacksonville. In fixing the time limit there was ample time for the Dauntless to reach Conception Island, where she transferred her Cubans to the schooner and towed the schooner to Orange Key, which was a more convenient place from which to complete the expedition. Then O'Brien hurried off to Jacksonville.

The next voyage of the Dauntless began innocently enough. She towed the schooner Jennie Thomas to Savannah. This was the ploy for leaving Jacksonville. She was searched and cleared on the St. Johns before reaching the bar. Getting her cargo and passengers at sea, she made a run to Cape Lucrecia for her landing. Midway through the debarkation, a Spanish ship appeared and the Dauntless left with some of its cargo still aboard. She arrived in Jacksonville on 2 December 1897, and conducted legitimate business until 12 February 1898.

When the tug departed Jacksonville in February, she stopped to pick up the cargo left from the Cape Lucrecia expedition before going to Fernandina for the Cubans and arms for this expedition. She landed half the cargo at point Nuevas Grandes, and the remainder the next night at Matanzas.

When the *Dauntless* returned to Jacksonville on 27 February her filibustering days were over. She was libeled for violating the neutrality laws, and a U.S. marshal was put on board. The situation changed with the blowing up of the USS *Maine* in Havana on 15 February, and the United States' declaration of war on 25 April 1898. A week before the war began, the Associated Press posted bond to use the *Dauntless* as a dispatch boat between Cuba and the United States.[23]

The role of Jacksonville as a filibustering port for the Cuban revolution was significant. There were seventy-one expeditions from the United States between 1895 and 1898; twenty-three of these attempts came from Jacksonville; only twenty-seven were successful, and twelve of the successful ones were made by the Jacksonville tugs *Three Friends*, *Commodore*, and *Dauntless*. In spite of the fact that the filibusters had the support of the American public, the U.S. government was successful in stopping these actions. There were forty-four unsuccessful attempts: the United States turned back thirty-three; the Spanish stopped five; the English halted two; and storms accounted for four failures.[24] As for the Cuban juntas in the United States, Dynamite Johnny O'Brien noted in his memoirs that Huau and Fritot "sacrificed more for the Cuban cause and rendered it more efficient service than did the delegation in New York," although the New York junta had the best publicity.[25]

Chapter Twelve

COASTAL DEFENSE:
St. Johns Bluff

In the 1880s the nation's strategic military planners made a series of studies to evaluate and to modernize the country's military posture. Out of this endeavor came a new concept of how to prepare coastal defenses. The following decade, with the advent of the Spanish-American War, the civic leaders in Jacksonville called upon the federal government to provide adequate defenses for their port and city. The result was the creation of a military reservation, the building of gun emplacements at St. Johns Bluff, and the mining of the river some eighteen miles downstream from Jacksonville.

In the decade after the Civil War, the United States military services reverted to near pre-1861 size and returned to peacetime duties. For the navy this meant showing the flag aboard sailing vessels built for extended cruising. For the army it meant a return to border patrols and Indian pacification on the western frontier. The recently developed military technologies of steam power, high-powered rifled guns, and armored protection were no longer needed. This period of military somnambulism continued until the 1880s, until Congress determined to take action to modernize the navy. But following on the discussions about the offensive potential of the new navy came the realization that coastal defense was the other side of the nation's military modernization coin.

In March 1885, the Endicott Board was charged to investigate and recommend the proper coastal defense for the country. It proposed a ring of fortifications around the United States. Concrete gun emplacements partially buried in the earth were the central feature of these defensive works. Armament would be powerful rifled guns and mortars. Fire-control posts, underground magazines, mines, electric searchlights, and smaller-caliber, rapid-firing guns would protect these installations from capture by an enemy shore party. The Endicott Board's new strategy centered upon weapons, as opposed to the earlier emphasis upon structures. [1]

The incentive to build coastal defenses increased after the Cuban Revolution against Spain began in 1895. Europeans engaging in combat ninety miles off Florida highlighted the thesis of our defenseless coasts. Early in 1898 the United States sent the USS *Maine* to Havana to protect American interests. On 15 February the *Maine* mysteriously exploded and sank in port with a loss of 260 sailors. Both nations prepared for war.

When Secretary of War Russell A. Alger learned of Spain's actions, he wrote: "The calls made upon the department for immediate rescue from the advancing Spanish fleet were pathetic in their urgency. Telegrams, letters, and statesmen representing the imperiled localities poured into the War Department. They wanted guns everywhere; mines in all the rivers and harbors on the map."[2]

In November 1897, long before the rest of the nation was gripped in the panic of foreign invasion, Governor William D. Bloxham wrote to the secretary of the navy requesting a loan of a light one-pounder Hotchkiss rapid-fire gun complete with field and boat mount for Florida's Naval Militia. He asked that the gun be sent on a Clyde line steamship to Jacksonville in care of Lieutenant Alexander R. Merrill, commanding the 3rd Division. [3]

On 20 February 1898, five days after the *Maine* sank, Governor Bloxham issued military orders to the Jacksonville Naval Militia to "make a reconnaissance of the Atlantic coast as far as practicable with a view to locating proper sites for signal stations and to secure such other data as may be obtained and be of value from a military standpoint."[4] Upon receipt of these orders Lt. Merrill began his survey at the mouth of the St. Johns River.

War rumors ran rife in Jacksonville, and there was great concern for the safety of the town. Not only had the port been a prime source of supplies for the Cuban rebels, but older citizens remembered that Jacksonville had been occupied four times during the Civil War. Each occupation began with navy gunboats escorting army transports up the St. Johns River. Thus, when the district engineer, Lieutenant Colonel William H. H. Benyaurd, was in town, newspaper reporters kept clamoring to be told about the plans to mine the river to protect the city. Benyaurd claimed no knowledge of mines being sent to Jacksonville.[5]

When Brigadier General John M. Wilson, Chief of Engineers, visited the city on 6 March 1898, many suspected that he was conducting a military inspection of the mouth of the river. When asked, the General replied that he had heard more rumors of war in Jacksonville than he had in Washington. Yet he insisted that he was in town to inspect the river's jetties. In fact, his boat trip on the tug *Martha Helen* to the jetties was in the company of R. G. Ross, one of the principal contractors for building the jetties. The General said nothing about defending the river.[6]

Defense continued to be a major topic in Jacksonville. In mid-March the *Times-Union & Citizen* had an intriguing article on mine defense. It reported that an "unnamed prominent citizen" had said that he was prepared to mine the St. Johns River himself. He claimed he knew how, and that he had the cables to do so. Toward the end of the month a group of active citizens appointed ex-Congressman Charles M. Cooper and W. W. Cummer to go to Washington, D.C., to impress upon the authorities the importance of protecting the town.[7]

The demand for military fortifications for the St. Johns River increased. On 2 April, General Wilson met with the secretary of war and some citizens from Jacksonville who had come to ask for guns and fortifications for their port. Cooper, Cummer, and

Congressman R. W. Davis said that the city would provide the mines and accessories for the support of the battery.

After the two officials agreed to the proposal, C. M. Cooper sent the following telegram: "Washington, D.C. April 2—J. H. Durkee, Jacksonville, Fla. We have orders for guns and mines—immediately from the Secretary of War. Colonel Benyaurd has been directed to confer with you." On 6 April, Cooper and Cummer were back in town with information that two modern rapid-fire five-inch guns, a secondary battery of other guns, and mines were destined for the St. Johns.[8]

It was 4 April before General Wilson telegraphed Colonel Benyaurd about the agreed fortifications for the St. Johns River. Benyaurd, in Miami, received orders to "cooperate at once with citizens of Jacksonville in reference to torpedo defense; select a site for four modern siege guns," and later to cooperate "with J. H. Durkee and others for submarine work to be done by them under your direction."[9]

The citizens of Jacksonville settled on St. Johns Bluff, eighteen miles downriver on the south bank, as the site to defend their port without consulting Colonel Benyaurd. The Colonel, in Miami, planned to meet with the people of Jacksonville on Thursday, 7 April. Yet on Monday, 4 April, two of the landowners on St. Johns Bluff wrote letters to Colonel Benyaurd granting the government the right to construct temporary fortifications on their land in return for an annual rental. Later, a third wrote in the same vein. Thus, even before Colonel Benyaurd arrived in Jacksonville, the citizens had selected the site and obtained the owners' permission to use their land. Thursday, 7 April, Benyaurd met with the Jacksonville committee, received the letters, and returned to his headquarters at St. Augustine.[10]

The following day Benyaurd telegraphed John Einig in Jacksonville asking to rent his tug *Edith*, and to have it ready for him the next day at the Main Street wharf. He also telegraphed John M. Cook of Spartanburg, South Carolina, offering him superintendency, with a salary of $125 per month, over the construction of a temporary battery. Work began on the harbor defenses on 11

April 1898, when John Cook led his civilian laborers to St. Johns Bluff to clear away the underbrush.[11]

The day after Cook began clearing the bluff, Benyaurd reached an agreement with William A. MacDuff of Jacksonville to build a landing wharf and four small temporary buildings close by for $531.63. Even before the wharf was completed, Cook began work on the temporary battery. Cook used 10-by-10-inch timbers in the revetment and magazine, which he covered with a sand embankment partly surfaced with "marsh muck."[12]

On 12 April, the Florida Central & Peninsula Railroad brought gun carriages into its yard at the foot of Julia Street. A number of people turned out to look at the carriages, and they were amused by some of the inscriptions written on the frames. "This will be no bullfight," was one comment, and another said: "For Blood-thirsty Spaniards." The people were relieved after see-ing these instruments of war sitting in their town, waiting to be installed downriver to protect them from marauding Spaniards.[13]

In mid-April, Colonel Benyaurd reported that he had decided to lay a railroad track from the boat landing up the bluff and use a stationary engine to haul the material to the top. (The Corps of Engineers sketch indicates that the tracks from the riverbank went up a ravine, or a man-made cut, to the top of the bluff.)[14]

Colonel Benyaurd met with Jacksonville citizens on 15 April and received quite a shock. When he asked them for a progress report on the city's mine defense program, all he got were blank stares. The committee was quick to claim, almost in unison, that it was under the impression that the government was providing everything for the mine field. Benyaurd, well along on his bat-tery construction, knew that without a mine field there would be a terrible weakness in his defenses. He immediately began order-ing the necessary material and lining up local support in order to lay the mines.

Benyaurd ordered eighteen hundred pounds of dynamite from C. B. Smith of Jacksonville. Then the colonel talked with Ben-jamin F. Dillon, the general manager of the Western Union Tele-graph Company, to find someone familiar with electric cables.

Dillon offered to place at his disposal his "principal cable man and electrician on two days notice." With that assurance, the colonel ordered two miles of submarine cable.[15]

When General Wilson learned that the city had done nothing about mining the St. Johns River, he wrote to the secretary of war and to Congressman R. W. Davis to inform them of this failure. Wilson reminded them that when they met with the citizens of Jacksonville, it was the citizens who had suggested that they place the mines themselves, and Colonel Benyaurd had been instructed to cooperate with them.[16]

Although it had no direct relation to the mine problem of the St. Johns River, a week later Lt. A. R. Merrill received orders from the state to build signal stations along the east coast of Florida, beginning at Mt. Cornelia, a sixty-three–foot mound on Fort George Island. Then he was to erect stations at Cape Canaveral, Jupiter, and Cape Florida.[17]

On the morning of 22 April 1898, the long-awaited guns for the bluff arrived: two five-inch breech-loading rifles and two seven-inch breech-loading howitzers. Until the gun emplacements were ready they sat on the railroad siding. People came out to look, and left feeling secure.[18]

On 27 April 1898, General Wilson issued an order to build a permanent emplacement on St. Johns Bluff for two eight-inch breech-loading rifles. Benyaurd revised his plans, laid out lines for a new gunpit, extended the railroad track another twelve hundred feet, and drilled for water. The Corps fortification sketch done in 1898 shows the location and type of weapons proposed by the Board of Engineers. Farthest south, on the crest facing St. Johns Creek, lay the battery for two eight-inch breech-loading rifles. This last battery is the concrete emplacement which still stands today.[19]

The hectic pace of construction continued. As the temporary gun emplacement neared completion, the four guns were shipped downriver on a barge and mounted.[20] However, Benyaurd soon received orders to dismount his four guns and carriages and send them to Tampa. The guns, shipped on 18 May, were destined to be used by the Army Expeditionary Force being readied for the invasion of Cuba.

Shortly after the temporary battery was dismounted, four light twelve-pounder field guns from Jacksonville were brought down to provide some defense for the river. In truth, these guns were a poor substitute. The twelve-pounders were muzzle-loading, smoothbore guns first produced just after the Mexican war. These guns were outmoded and of no use against armored ships. Nevertheless, they were mounted in the emplacement with their muzzles pointing out from the earthen embankment, providing a threatening appearance. [21]

Early in May, Colonel Benyaurd requested more money for his mine defense program. Originally he had hoped that the Florida Naval Militia would patrol the mine field. Although the Naval Militia had built the signal station on Mt. Cornelia, it had not been accepted for mine patrol work. Therefore, Benyaurd had to pay for boats and civilian personnel to patrol the mine field. [22]

From the records it is apparent that Colonel Benyaurd was not informed of the duties of the Florida Naval Militia. Other than acknowledging that it had built the signal station on Mt. Cornelia, he made no mention of the fact that the militia manned the station throughout the fighting. In all probability, the lack of communication between the signal station and the fortifications at St. Johns Bluff may be due to the fact that, throughout this period, the bluff was under the control of civilian workers of the Corps of Engineers. At no time during the history of the military reservation at St. Johns Bluff were troops assigned to the fortifications. [23]

It was ironic that at the end of the month, just as Lt. W. M. Harts completed his mine field, the U.S. Navy discovered and bottled up the Spanish fleet in Santiago, Cuba, which eliminated the need for defenses on the St. Johns River. Harts received twenty-one cases of buoyant mines, which he loaded with a hundred pounds of dynamite per case. True to his word, Dillon sent his two men to supervise the laying of the submarine cable which connected the mines in the river to the mine casemate.

The mines were divided into sets of threes. Five sets were placed in the river on either side of the channel. The remaining two sets were loaded, but kept in readiness to be placed across the open channel, if the occasion should demand.

During the mining operations some vessels interfered with the small boats placing the mines. On several occasions the passing ships actually cut the cables. When Harts complained, Colonel Benyaurd telegraphed J.H. Durkee, asking him to inform the St. Johns River pilots that they must be more careful. The colonel did not mince words: "Vessels are violating my published regulations regarding mines by cutting cables and disengaging the system[.] If not immediately discontinued I will have pilots licenses revoked."[24] Benyaurd received no more complaints.

Colonel Benyaurd's navigation regulations hindered normal ship activity because passage to Jacksonville could only take place during daylight. Further, no vessel could come through the jetties or down the river late in the day and anchor at Mayport overnight.[25]

On the morning of 10 June 1898, John J. O'Rourke, the electrician from the Western Union office in Jacksonville, his helper, an African-American named Hogart, and a laborer, Edward Houston, were in the temporary mine casemate on the bluff checking some of the mine plugs (fuses in present-day terminology). The casemate was a building sixteen by twenty-five feet which held the terminals of the submarine cables to the planted mines, and several batteries. In the building with them were Lt. Harts and Thomas S. Bonham, his stenographer. O'Rourke, Hogart, and Houston were at one end of the room while Harts and Bonham were in the center of the casemate. Harts had his back to O'Rourke as he dictated letters. Hogart asked Houston to fill in for him while he stepped outside for a break. A few minutes later O'Rourke passed Houston a mine plug to hold while he tested it by passing a weak current through it. For some unknown reason, O'Rourke touched the plug with a cable carrying a full current. The explosion blew Houston to pieces, killed O'Rourke instantly, and sent shrapnel into the head and back of Lt. Harts, who survived his injuries. Neither Bonham nor Hogart was in-jured, but the wooden building was destroyed.

Benjamin Dillon could not understand how it could have hap-pened. O'Rourke was his chief electrician and his principal cable constructor. He had been with the company as an electrician for fifteen years. Dillon just shook his head in disbelief. O'Rouke and Houston were the only casualties of the mine field during the war.[26]

A week after the peace protocol was signed, Colonel Benyaurd lifted his navigation restrictions on the river. He told the collec-tor of the port that the "mines will be removed or exploded as soon as Capt [R. P.] Johnston [he had relieved Lt. Harts] returns from Tampa. Meantime the Corps of Engineers will continue to guide ships through channel."[27]

Captain Johnston deactivated the mine field during the early weeks of September by exploding the fifteen mines rather than risk an accidental explosion and injuries by trying to retrieve and disarm the cases, which had been submerged for over three months. The six loaded reserve mines, not submerged, were dis-armed. Until all the submerged mines had been exploded, Johnston kept up his boat patrol.

When Captain Johnston recovered the cable from the mine field, he had nine reels of single and multiple cable. These reels, weighing about nine hundred pounds each, were kept submerged in the river, moored alongside the wharf. On 2 October 1898, a severe northeaster struck the region and several of the reels broke loose and were partially buried in the sand. Johnston hired a diver to find the reels and put lines on them. The next time the Corps' snagboat *Suwannee* came to Jacksonville, she raised the reels and placed them in a small creek near the bluff for safekeeping.[28]

Meanwhile, there was still a high priority placed on complet-ing the eight-inch gun emplacements. In September a rock crusher was rented in Jacksonville to increase the supply of crushed stones for the bluff. Steamers and lighters carried the stone downriver. In November John Cook told Colonel Benyaurd that he would need more money if he were to continue construction on the emplacement. Benyaurd told him that the guns must be mounted, but since the war was over he could not increase the funding for the project. He suggested that Cook might have to lower the height planned for the concrete pit, and that it was not necessary to install the heavy metal doors called for in the plans. In other words, he instructed Cook to cut corners, but get the work done as soon as possible.[29]

In January 1899, the two eight-inch breech-loading rifles, each weighing 32,480 pounds, were mounted at the top of St. Johns Bluff. Each gun fired a 300-pound projectile capable of penetrating 10.6 inches of steel at thirty-five hundred yards. The concrete cover over the magazines had not been finished, nor had sand been placed over the magazines, but the war had ended a month earlier and further work on St. Johns Bluff was suspended.[30] Similar to the fate of the earlier guns on the bluff, these guns were never serviced by troops nor test-fired by the Corps' civilian employees.

In March 1899, three months after the peace treaty had been signed, Colonel Benyaurd asked the Merrill-Stevens Engineering Co. to submit a bid for removing nine reels of cable from St. Johns Bluff and carrying it to Jacksonville to be loaded on a train. J. E. Merrill replied that it would cost two hundred dollars because the wooden spools which held the wire were damaged. The company would have to repair the spools prior to moving the cable to ensure that the wire would not fall off in transit. This was done and the reels were shipped to the cable storage tank in Tampa.[31]

When Benyaurd's tour of duty in Florida was over, he was relieved by Captain Charles H. McKinstry, who had been in charge of the fortifications and mines at Key West during the war. Initially, McKinstry spent a good deal of time studying Benyaurd's correspondence and records to acquaint himself with the situation at St. Johns Bluff. His first concern was the mines and dynamite at the bluff. When he found that a foreign mine had been picked up in the river near the bluff over a year earlier, he instructed Charles Sperry, his overseer at Mayport, to find it, examine it, and describe it to him. From Sperry's report, McKinstry concluded that "the mine in question is undoubtedly one of our own and has drifted from somewhere up the coast." He told Sperry not to take off the cap, but to explode a pound of dynamite at the mine's lowering ring; then, if there were any remains, to dispose of them in some place where they would not obstruct navigation. McKinstry's last words were: "Remember this is dangerous—take precautions."

A week later Sperry wrote: "I exploded the torpedo today by an electric current through its own fuses. Nothing was found of the torpedo afterwards, except about a square foot of its shell." This ended McKinstry's mine scare, and the port of Jacksonville's problems with mines during the Spanish-American War.[32] Today, the huge concrete eight-inch gun emplacement and magazine storage rooms are the only remains of the Spanish-American War fortifications at St. Johns Bluff, and this memorial is surrounded by residential homes on the bluff.

Chapter Thirteen

TOPOGRAPHICAL CHANGES

The development of Jacksonville's maritime interests wrought considerable topographical changes to the river and the beaches fronting the port. The turning point appeared in the 1880s. Before that time, nature was the impetus for change; since that time, man-made maritime projects have been added to the transitional forces. At all times, northeast storms and hurricanes have overridden the less spectacular natural and man-made alterations. Of course, Florida's beaches have always been in a transitory state, shifting at the whim of winds, tides, and storms. Deputy Surveyor H. S. Duval recorded the natural changes to the beaches in 1882 when he surveyed the Andrew Dewees tract.

The most nefarious of Andrew Dewees's heirs, according to Duval, "was a son-in-law [actually grandson-in-law] of old Dewees named Cornelius Taylor he is represented as a pirate and fearful murderer, in which his wife was his confederate. He became possessed of the whole grant or most of it. Some say by fraud, and murder, as he murdered one or more of his brother-in-laws, and finally his wife, and married his wife's sister (if I am rightly informed). [In 1841] he finally sold out to [David L.] Palmer & [Darius] Ferris and disappeared."[1]

Regardless of the truth of all of Duval's comments, other heirs challenged Taylor's disposal of the Dewees grant. In December

1882 Duval resurveyed the tract, except for the portion sold to Palmer and Ferris, which had become Mayport. Accompanied by two of the disputant heirs, Joseph F. Floyd and A. B. Floyd, Duval began at a pine tree marked with a cross and long known to be the base point between Dewees's claim to the north and Don Juan McQueen's grant to the south.[2]

Duval's survey provides the opportunity to note the changing shape of the beaches from the Spanish survey of 1792 to 1882. Normally one is accustomed to think of land change as a slow, imperceptible process involving geologic, not historic, time; such as, mountains eroding, or rivers gouging canyons. But the interface of sandy land and sea is a constantly changing region, as Duval noted while comparing his work with earlier surveys.

Duval didn't believe the Spanish surveyor actually ran his southern line, for he recorded that it was 130 chains long, while Duval's survey had 149.30 chains from the pine tree to the beach. (One chain equals sixty-six feet.) Duval could not believe that the beach had grown over a thousand feet in ninety years. Still, he had to admit that from the 130-chain mark a line at right angles to the north for 195 chains would "just about reach to where in all probability the initial point of the Spanish Survey stood."[3]

Duval turned north along the coast and encountered the opposite phenomenon. Up the beach for several miles erosion had caused the seaward side of the sandhills to be perpendicular, with logs "buried probably for ages" sticking out. Crossing Taylor's road, he recorded it was Cornelius Taylor's "dead line for any one who settled South of it was shot." At another place he observed that a marsh described in the Spanish survey was disappearing as the sand blowing from the sandhills filled in the area. "The trees and bushes now growing up in it, and surrounded by marsh grass, will soon destroy the grass, and in the course of time be one continuous wood."[4]

The most impressive land erosion took place at the mouth of the St. Johns River. Duval recorded a foot bridge, recently destroyed during a storm, buried in the sand. Just north of that was a Confederate gun battery which had been washed into the sea. He also sketched in more land which had washed away in the previous fifty years. This land formerly had been the sites of two lighthouses at the mouth of the St. Johns.

Navigational lights at the mouth of the St. Johns provide another example of the changes wrought by sand and water on man's onshore buildings. In 1828, Congress set aside sixty-five hundred dollars to build the first lighthouse. The site selected was Generals Mound, at the very mouth of the river. But when the mound turned out to be just a sandhill, the site was moved inland behind the mound, and about a hundred feet from high water. In 1830, this lighthouse began operations. A northeasterly gale struck the coast in 1832, and the following January a committee reported: "The bank which is about 12 feet high has worn away to within the distance of 4 feet of the dwelling, the brick of which the cistern is composed is already exposed." The following year, the Lighthouse Board issued a contract for a new lighthouse midway between San Pablo Creek and the beach, and set back 689 feet from the highwater mark.[5]

By 1852 the St. Johns River encroached upon the second lighthouse. Ship captains complained that the shifting sand dune had almost covered the keeper's house, and the same dune obscured the light as their ships drew near to the beach. A year later Dr. Able S. Baldwin wrote to both the Corps of Engineers and the Lighthouse Board stressing the dangers of high water to the lighthouse.[6] Then the Lighthouse Board learned that Cornelius Taylor's title to the lighthouse reservation had not been clear when he sold the land to the government. Finally, when Lieutenant Horatio C. Wright recommended that a new site be selected, the board went to Congress for funds to build a third lighthouse at the mouth of the St. Johns River, and on 1 January 1859, this new lighthouse became operational.[7]

In 1887 the new lighthouse was raised another fifteen feet. Then in 1912 the candle power was increased fifteen times. Finally, in 1929, the light was abandoned in favor of a lightship. The Coast Guard anchored the *St. Johns Lightship* eight miles east of the bar. In 1953, a new lighthouse was built a mile south of the jetties on the Coast Guard Base at Mayport. It is rated as a fifteen-mile light, but ship captains claim to have seen it twenty-five miles out to sea.[8]

The 1880s were a pivotal decade in the shaping of the beaches. Earlier changes had been natural, depending upon the elements to alter the topography. This decade saw the impact of man upon the land and its surrounding waterways. Over the following decades, engineering projects deepened, straightened, and fixed the St. Johns River's channel to the sea; dredged an intracoastal waterway, separating the beaches from the mainland; dug a ship basin to berth aircraft carriers; built groins and seawalls to stop beach erosion; and finally pumped sand to renourish eroded beaches. Hence, after 1880, man and nature shaped the beaches.

Mrs. W. E. Scull, an early resident of Jacksonville Beach, told of the disaster to Mayport from the effect of the "widening and deepening of the channel [which] caused the water to wash with great force behind the jetties. The summer cottages were washed into the ocean. The Atlantic House was moved back twice, the last time, away back on the high beach where the jetties started, but finally it, too, was washed away. [This Atlantic hotel is not to be confused with a later one which had formerly been the Continental Hotel at Atlantic Beach.] After the jetties were completed, that section filled up with soil, and no doubt in time there will be trees there on the Mayport side."[9]

There is a discrepancy in Mrs. Scull's account. According to her manuscript, the erosion from the jetties took place in 1876, but jetty construction did not take place until 1880, and she didn't move to the beach until 1884. In all probability 1876 is a typographical error and the proper date should be 1886.

Meanwhile, in August 1881, the Florida Coast Line & Transportation Company received a state charter to dredge a waterway from the St. Johns River to Miami. This project literally separated the beaches from the mainland of Florida; the beaches became an island. In 1923 the Florida Coast Line & Transportation Company went into receivership. New owners took over just as the south Florida land boom began. Two years later the demand from south Florida was great enough for the canal company to record a profit. When the land boom burst, the new company went into receivership, and the canal into disrepair. [10]

Unfortunately for the prospective canal users, the Florida Coast Line & Transportation Company provided little maintenance once a section had been dredged, examined, accepted by the state, and the granted land turned over to the company. In 1926 Colonel Gilbert A. Youngberg of the Corps of Engineers said that the canal's "dimensions have never been successfully maintained, and, except by taking advantage of tides and high waters, navigation with vessels of more than 4-foot draft is practically impossible."[11] In 1927 the Florida Inland Navigation District issued bonds to finance the purchase of the right-of-way from the canal company in anticipation of turning the private waterway over to the federal government as a part of its intracoastal waterway system. In December 1929 the Corps took possession of the waterway. [12]

Colonel Laurence V. Frazier assumed control of the waterway with instructions from Congress to create a canal seventy-five feet wide and eight feet deep. With the precision of a military assault operation, he sent the United States Sangboat D-1 into Pablo Creek, heading south to remove obstructions. The U.S. pipeline dredge *Congree* followed in the wake of the D-1, removing fill from the channel. Frazier sent the leased pipeline dredge *Simons* up from St. Augustine to work its way north to meet the D-1 and the *Congree*. Ahead of the *Simons* the leased derrick boat *Joeb* raised snags. [13]

In the 1930s the people of Jacksonville Beach became interested in the intracoastal waterway. When the Florida East Coast Railway stopped its service to the beach in 1932, goods could reach Jacksonville Beach either by truck along Atlantic Boulevard or by barge. The barge route from Jacksonville followed the St. Johns River to the intracoastal waterway, then south to the Atlantic Boulevard crossing where the goods were transshipped by truck the remaining five and a half miles to Jacksonville Beach.

In 1933 the Brown Boat Line, which operated shallow-draft freight boats from Jacksonville to Vero Beach along the intracoastal waterway, refused eight carloads of freight for Jacksonville Beach "because of the lack of docking facilities."[14] This spurred the local officials to request federal aid. Jacksonville Beach wanted a turning basin off the intracoastal waterway.

By 1945 the city council of Jacksonville Beach had provided the rights-of-way and the spoil disposal area, but the Florida State Road Department made plans to construct what later became Beach Boulevard. By the time the boulevard opened to the public on 14 December 1949, the need for docking facilities had diminished, and no actions were taken to implement the Jacksonville Beach turning basin.

The intracoastal waterway never did become a commercial thoroughfare because of the rail and highway competition. However, today the waterway is a major artery for recreational boats traveling north and south along the east coast, following the appropriate seasons. This had led to the development of marina facilities at the mouth of the St. Johns catering to this traffic. In addition, more than a few of the passing boaters make a side trip upriver to Jacksonville.

In the forties, land at the northern end of the beaches was dredged to provide a naval base. An early map (ca. 1830) showed a pond just inland from the mouth of the St. Johns whose exit was a marsh creek running into San Pablo Creek. Evidently, over the years, the erosion of the southern riverbank reached the pond, which became known as Ribault Bay (although it did not exist in 1562 when the French explorer examined the river).

In 1939, the United States Navy wanted to create a carrier docking basin at Mayport to support the aircraft squadrons based in northeast Florida. In April 1941, Congress appropriated a million dollars to commence dredging. A month later plans were changed, canceling the carrier berth and creating a crash and patrol boat facility.[15] Six months later, the Jacksonville Times-Union devoted a full page of photographs to the changes being wrought to Ribault Bay as the navy's Mayport station took shape.

On 15 December 1944, the USS *Guadalcanal* (CVE-60), an escort aircraft carrier, steamed into Mayport's crash and patrol boat facility and tied up to the mooring buoy in the center of the basin. At times there was less than a foot between the carrier's hull and the bottom of the basin. The *Guadalcanal* was the precursor of Mayport's future role as a carrier basin. From this date until 1 September 1945, when she was relieved by the USS *Solomons* (CVE-67), she engaged in training cruises off Mayport and in the Caribbean, and during the last five months the *Guadalcanal* performed as a carrier qualifications ship for the area's naval aviators.[16]

In 1950, plans for the carrier basin were reactivated. Contracts were issued for constructing a carrier pier on the north side of the basin, dredging the basin to forty feet, and extending and improving the runway. By 1952 the Mayport Naval Station had a carrier basin of two thousand-by three thousand-feet, and the community of Mayport found itself nearly surrounded by a major fleet installation.

When Captain Jack P. Monroe, USN, brought the first carrier, the USS *Tarawa* (CVA-40), into Mayport after it had become a carrier basin, his approach seemed déjà vu, for his scheduled arrival on 27 October had to be delayed three days because of high winds and strong currents in the channel. On the fourth day, Captain Vernon A. Davis, the civilian pilot, brought the *Tarawa* into the basin under perfect conditions.[17]

Recently, beach erosion, a natural process in operation since time immemorial, became a concern of the beach communities. Tides, waves, littoral drift, and inlet currents all are prime movers of sand beaches. These forces rearrange the sand on Florida's shoreline. Total beach area may remain relatively stable, but the location of the transitory beaches shifts.[18]

However, much of recent erosion has been man-made, not only by maritime projects, but by dune destruction as the land is leveled to erect structures at the very land edge of the beach. Local interests have long maintained that the jetty work intensified the erosion south of the river's mouth, and they point to Talbot

Island's extension of nine thousand feet south due to sand accretion.[19] This sand buildup was caused by the river current disrupting the natural southern littoral drift, but the jetties have increased the effectiveness of the river's barrier.

In addition to the erosion caused by the jetties, hurricanes and severe storms wreak havoc upon beaches. Huge wave actions, especially during high tides, smash the shoreline, washing away large areas at an unbelievable rate. A century's work of building a sandy beach may be swept away during five to ten hours of battering under storm conditions.

In 1978 the first beach renourishment project began. Initially it had been planned to use the dredged material from routine harbor dredging of the St. Johns River, but later it was decided to use a borrow area at sea four to six miles offshore. The task ended in October 1980, when over three million cubic yards of sand had been put on ten miles of beach.[20] Unfortunately for the plan, storm damage was excessive in the years immediately following the project, and the whole program must begin again sooner than expected. This has led to some questioning of the soundness of the original plan. Thus, at the end of the first century of man-made influences on topographical change, the familiar process whereby one change leads to another problem continues to unfold.

Chapter Fourteen

FIRE AND WARS

Of course, there were other shipbuilders and shipping interests in Jacksonville besides the Merrill-Stevens company and the Clyde Line, but these two were the bellwethers of the port. And, in ways reminiscent of the filibustering days, some people within the port engaged in rum-running during the prohibition years. The actions of these two companies and of the bootleggers demonstrate the vitality and versatility of the maritime interests of the port during these trying times.

In 1887 the Merrill brothers, J. Eugene and Alexander, teamed up with their friend Arthur Stevens to incorporate the Merrill-Stevens Engineering Company. The company prospered and built its reputation by the diversity of its undertakings. During the 1890s it fashioned the ironwork for the Duval County jail, repaired fire engines, built over a hundred boilers for ships steaming on local waters, and designed and built wood and steel steamboats.

One of Merrill-Stevens's contemporary advertisements showed a small, square-stern paddlewheel steamboat under the statement, "One Man Can Run This Steamboat." The pilothouse was just aft of the bow, next to it was the steam boiler, then the boxy cabin running back to the paddlewheel. The vessel was 37 feet long, 9.5 foot beam, 2 feet depth of hold, drew 12 inches of water, and cruised at 8 miles an hour. The cabin was 14 feet long, 9 feet wide, and 6.5 feet high. It had two folding beds and a galley. These steamboats could be configured for pleasure, to carry light freight, or for commercial fishing. The nominal cost was twelve hundred dollars, but the company was willing to alter its basic design to the owner's needs at prices ranging from nine hundred to fifteen hundred dollars.[1]

Sometime toward the end of the decade, as noted in the company's letterhead, Merrill-Stevens bought out the Jacksonville Marine Railway, across the river on the south bank. This acquisition brought to the company the largest marine railway in Florida, and it allowed Merrill-Stevens to haul the four-masted lumber schooners, the biggest ships on the river, onto its ways.

The spring of 1901 was dry. On 3 May a disaster struck Jacksonville just after noon. The Cleveland Fibre Factory processed moss. The moss was soaked in large vats first and then spread out on platforms to dry. In one of the nearby cabins, a cook, preparing the noon meal, stoked the fire and some burning cinders rose up the chimney. Factory employees sitting in the drying yard eating lunch smelled smoke. Upon investigation, they found a number of fires smoldering in the drying moss. They began stamping out the fires. But about the same time the westerly wind stiffened and the smoldering moss burst into flames. The ensuing attempts to stamp out the fires only aggravated the situation. Soon a number of burning wads of moss, carried on the freshening wind, drifted into the factory. Here they settled on the dry moss waiting to be soaked, and immediately the flames grew larger and reached toward the dry wooden shingled roof.

The foreman called the fire department as soon as the first burning wads swept into the factory, and the firemen answered promptly. But the fire chief doubted if he could control the now raging inferno. At 1:00 P.M. he ordered a general alarm as the whole factory blazed. The heat generated inside the building became intense, and as the superheated air rose it carried burning moss, shingles, and other blazing fragments aloft to be wafted eastward by the wind. These incendiaries settled back to earth among the nearby wooden homes, where the process repeated itself and grew more violent by the minute.

The fire raced eastward into the heart of downtown Jacksonville. By now people were filling the streets, at first to look, then to help the firemen, and finally to gather their loved ones and what belongings they could and flee. The sky rained fire, and as the burning zone increased in size, the heat radiating outward downwind overran the falling embers. As the fire reached the center of town, the intense wall of heat was several hundred feet ahead of the falling embers preparing the way for the firestorm.

At about five o'clock the wind shifted to the north and the inferno changed its course to travel southward toward the St. Johns River. The waterfront, which had been relatively safe before the wind changed, now became the object of the flames. Again the heat wall preceded the fire, now moving south. The hot rising air actually was strong enough to create several water spouts on the river. Fortunately for those on the river, no damage resulted from the turbulent air which sucked water skyward.

At 7:30 P.M. the wind died down, and an hour later the fire was under control. In eight hours 146 city blocks (466 acres) were burned, 2,368 buildings were destroyed, 8,677 people were left homeless, and 7 lives were lost. The heat had been so intense that there were no charred remains in the devastated area, just white ash where the flammable objects had been consumed in Jacksonville's Great Fire of 1901.[2]

The Merrills put fleeing refugees in their boats and sent them to the south bank for safety. They worked all afternoon and into the night ferrying people away from the holocaust, even as their shipyard was consumed by the flames.[3]

Personnel of the Clyde Line also pitched in to aid the victims of the fire. The captain of the ship in port at the outset of the fire remained at the wharf and opened his gangway to take aboard all who came to him. He made the galley available for his crew to feed the refugees. He even steamed away from the wharf several times to go upriver to give the people an opportunity to breathe fresh air.

The line had two wharves in downtown Jacksonville; the Hogan Street one escaped the fire, but the one at the foot of Washington Street was burned. When the *Frederick DeBary*, one of the line's river boats, arrived in Jacksonville, it, too, opened its gangway to the refugees. Later the Clyde Line donated considerable money to aid the citizens in need. And as one ship would depart Jacksonville, another would take its place, acting as a shelter for the needy.[4]

One of the amazing aftermaths of the fire was the rapidity with which the business community turned to rebuild. Sam P. Holmes was credited with being the first. According to the story, Holmes remarked to the onlookers during the fire: "Boys, I will begin rebuilding tomorrow." In fact, he is supposed to have hired laborers the night of the fire to report to him the next day to begin the rebuilding. Saturday morning his crew could be seen pouring water on the hot bricks to cool them so that they could be handled.[5]

The Merrill-Stevens Engineering Company also rebuilt, and in an ad in the City Directory of 1903 the company related some of its accomplishments since the fire. The steamers *Elam*, *City of Fayetteville*, *Vagabond*, and *Three Kids*, the barges *Cameron* and *Ralston*, the schooner *Pargo*, and two launches had been built. The ad said that the company now specialized in yacht repairs and was ready to design and build houseboats. This was an amazing display of recovery.[6]

In the year after the 1903 ad, the company built the steamer *Washington A. Clark*, the Corps of Engineers snagboat the *Florida*, and the ferryboat *Duval*. This last vessel bridged the St. Johns River from its terminus at the foot of Main Street. In 1904, when the United States began construction on the Panama Canal, Merrill-Stevens built and delivered to Colón, Panama, eleven steel barges.[7]

Two years later, in 1906, Merrill-Stevens built a forty-five hundred–ton dry dock. This allowed the company to handle ships up to six thousand tons, and it was the largest dry dock south of Cape Hatteras. The *Agnus Manning* was the first ocean-going vessel to use this dry dock. She was a four-masted schooner whose keel had been torn off when she went aground on the beach near the St. Johns bar.[8]

By 7 July 1910, the Clyde Line had outgrown its piers and it began construction on a new terminal. Less than a year later, in May 1911, the terminal opened to the public. It was functionally designed. Two large sheds were built on two separate piers; each pier was 450 feet long and 150 feet wide. Railroad spur tracks ran into each shed. The eastern shed carried freight for New York. The western shed held goods bound for Boston. The northern shed, connecting the two piers along the riverfront, held local freight. The second floor was for passengers and held the shipping offices. This whole complex enclosed enough space to dock as many as six ships at a time.[9]

The Merrill-Stevens Engineering Company was versatile. Prior to World War I, it built the *José Padrón* for the cattle trade out of Buenos Aires, Argentina. The *Padrón* was a steel hull sidewheeler with electric lights. *La Gloria* was a sternwheeler designed "with all the modern improvements" for the Cuban trade. The *Osceola* was a St. Johns riverboat. And the *Vagabondia* was a houseboat built for W. L. Mellon, the nephew of Andrew W. Mellon.

In addition to shipbuilding, J. Eugene Merrill was an innovator. He built the *William M. Tupper* for the Gulf Steamship Company, a subsidiary of the Clyde Line, on land. When it came time to launch the *Tupper*, she was moved on rollers to a dry dock first, and then she was launched from the dry dock. This system was later used when ships were mass-produced during World War II. Merrill was ahead of his time.[10]

When Arthur Stevens and Alexander Merrill sold their interest in the company in 1916, J. Eugene Merrill sought out other associates to join the company, which was reorganized as the Merrill-Stevens Shipbuilding Corporation.[11] That same year Kenneth Alexander Merrill joined his father in the business.

The United States' entry into World War I brought great change to the port. The shipbuilding business boomed, while the shipping portion of the port came to a standstill because of German submarines. On 3 June 1918, the Navy Department closed the port because of submarine attacks off the New Jersey coast. The Merchants & Miners Line canceled its ship scheduled to leave Jacksonville upon receipt of the navy's order. The Clyde Line's *Mohawk* cleared port before the navy's order, and it was called back by wireless. The *Arapahoe*, scheduled to come to Jacksonville, was held in its Carolina port. Later, some coastal shipping was allowed, but the Clyde Line embargoed all freight destined for New York and Boston because it had to pass through the area where enemy submarines lurked.[12]

Meanwhile, the government gave contracts to several Jacksonville shipbuilding companies besides Merrill-Stevens, including J. M. Murdock Company, Morey & Thomas, St. Johns River Shipbuilding Company, and A. Bentley & Sons, Inc. In all, about forty-two ships were built in Jacksonville. When the composite ship *Red Cloud* slid down the ways at Merrill-Stevens shipyard, it was the first composite ship built in the south. (A composite ship has steel frames to which are attached wooden planking.) The shipyard had another first when its workers completed laying the keel for the next ship just nine minutes after the *Red Cloud* had vacated the ways.[13]

During the war, Merrill-Stevens built five composite vessels, all 255 feet long with reciprocal steam engines. It also constructed five steel ships 325 feet long, which were turbine-driven. Three of these turbine-driven ships were later owned by the C. D. Mallory Company and continued in service until torpedoed during World War II.

Besides constructing ships from the keel up, the company converted several ships for new usage. The dredge *Atlantic* became a minesweeper for the French government, and a freighter was remodeled to become the *Larkspur*, a six hundred–bed hospital ship for the army. Many vessels underwent overhaul and repair in the Merrill-Stevens yard. The barge *Southeast* became the first concrete sheathed barge overhauled by the company. It was placed in dry dock, the bottom sheathed with metal laths, and then covered with concrete, another first for Southern shipbuilders.

With the end of the war, the roles between the two port businesses of shipbuilding and shipping reversed. The shipping lines resumed their carrying trade, while the shipyards found work to be at a premium. Merrill-Stevens shut down all of its southside yards and sold the property as it reverted to peacetime operations.[14]

Peace may have come to the business interests of the port, but the prohibition era, 1920–1933, brought quasi-wartime conditions to the Treasury Department's Coast Guard and Bureau of Prohibition, as well as to the local sheriffs and police officers. The Senate's 1931 study of the enforcement of Prohibition produced some general strategies followed by the bootleggers and by the Prohibition agents. For example, the normal procedure for bringing liquors into the United States by waterborne craft was to send a mother ship to a rendezvous point well out in international waters, where it would load fast speedboats for a run into an unprotected shore. The Great Lakes and Florida's east coast were close enough to foreign land to eliminate the need for a mother ship. Small craft could operate directly between the overseas port and the United States.

The Coast Guard countered these strategies by two lines of defense. It used small picket boats to watch the unprotected coast and the larger seventy-five–footers to seek out the offshore mother ships. Occasionally the larger Coast Guard vessel might hide near an island and send out small fast open boats at night to run into known inlets used by rumrunners. Often government lawmen relied upon tips from its own undercover agents, concerned law-abiding citizens, or members of rival bootleggers for the correct time to be at a specific landing.

Smugglers employed great ingenuity to avoid capture with incriminating goods in their possession. When chased in shallow waters by law enforcement agents, the bootlegger might throw his cargo over the side. Often a buoy was attached to the cases and weighted down with a bag of salt. It would take two or three days for the salt to dissolve and release its buoy. Later, the bootlegger would return to search the surface for his jettisoned cargo. An even more elaborate device was the submersible tank towed beneath the surface behind the rumrunner's boat. It was not likely to be discovered, and it, too, could be cut loose and recovered at a later time after the lawmen had gone.

Frank Buckley, of the Treasury's Bureau of Prohibition, painted a dismal picture of Jacksonville and its port:

> Jacksonville, second largest city in the State, leading lumber-port of the South, gateway to practically all tourist resorts in Florida, harbors, during the rush period, a vast transient population. In addition it houses that restless seafaring element characteristic of important maritime communities. The flow of the winter tourist flood naturally carries with it a large criminal tide that, for the most part, halts en route at Jacksonville. As a consequence, crime conditions in that city during the winter months are at a high point.[15]

In the Treasury Department's view of law enforcement, Jacksonville was unique. It lay far enough away from the Bahamas to warrant using mother ships to carry illegal liquor, yet close enough for specially adapted motorboats to make a direct transit. Thus agents operating out of the port of Jacksonville encountered all of the strategies mentioned in the Senate's voluminous report.

In the early hours of 4 June 1920, deputy sheriffs and city detectives raided the steamer *St. Johns County* tied up at the Merrill-Stevens dock and seized more than thirty gallons of expensive foreign liquor and arrested four Spanish sailors alleged to have brought in the illegal cargo.[16]

In October 1921, the yacht *Kona* tried to sneak into port one night, only to run aground on the rocks at the mouth of the jetties. The forty-three-ton boat was pounded to pieces by the sea, and one of the five crewmen lost his life in the disaster. When the other four reached Mayport, a Mr. "Smith" hustled them across the river to the north bank and then transported them into Jacksonville, where they were lost to all authorities. The paper reported that no one at Mayport would talk to its reporters about the shipwreck or the missing crew. However, by word of mouth, the news spread that the *Kona*'s cargo was washing up on the beach, and two hundred people visited the beaches and the wreck to gather the liquor. Those arriving early in boats got most of the cargo, but even late arrivals walking the beach at low tide could pick up a bottle or two. Authorities examined the *Kona*'s remains and determined that she had been modified to hold a larger, more powerful motor than most yachts.[17]

The crew of the British auxiliary schooner *Louise F.* told the most bizarre story when Treasury agents seized their ship off Pablo Beach. (In 1925 the state legislature changed the name from Pablo Beach to Jacksonville Beach.) The crewmen claimed that the schooner was bound from Nassau to Nova Scotia, well beyond the three-mile limit, when rum pirates came aboard and forced them to take the *Louise F.*, with its $375,000 liquor cargo, in to Pablo Beach. The twelve crewmen were held over for a federal grand jury. Two months later Sam Case, alias Arthur Foster, the second mate of the schooner, changed his plea to guilty. The remaining crewmen stuck by their story and alleged that Case's two accomplices had fled before being captured. They also said that they had off-loaded about twenty cases before the agents made their arrest. The judge evidently accepted this story, for only Case was sentenced to a year and a day in the federal penitentiary at Atlanta.[18]

In the quasi-war against the rumrunners, Sheriff W. H. Dowling used three boats during the first six months of 1924. His first boat was a converted submarine chaser, the *Russ*. Within three days Dowling captured two bootleggers. The *Skipper Bill*'s crew was busy off-loading at Pablo Beach when the sheriff and federal agents surprised and arrested them. Two days later Dowling received a tip that the *Manito II* would be in the St. Johns River with an illegal cargo. The *Manito* was also a former submarine chaser converted and outfitted as a private yacht. Dowling was on the river Monday night patrolling for the smugglers. When Dowling spotted his prey, the chase was on. The rumrunners were surprised to find that Dowling's *Russ* was as fast as their boat. Near Clapboard Creek the crew of the *Manito* beached their yacht on the mud bank and fled on foot. The *Manito*, with 150 cases of liquor aboard, was confiscated and later condemned in court. The paper stated that: "The boat is said to be owned by Dr. C. Curtis Collins, Jacksonville physician. According to the customs house records the master of record is Roger Ware."[19]

Sometime later the *Russ* blew up, several miles at sea off Mayport. Dowling's next boat was a small speedboat, which was wrecked when it was slammed against the jetties by a large wave. Several deputies, on board at the time, had to swim to the rocks for safety. In June Dowling had his third craft, another speedboat. By now he was working closely with the Coast Guard. After his men seized a $25,000 cache of liquor on the beach, Dowling reported this to the Coast Guard and the *Yamacraw* went out off the jetties to investigate. The captain of the cutter found two vessels loaded with liquor anchored about fifteen miles off Pablo Beach. Because the ships were in international waters beyond the limit stated in the Anglo-American Rumrunning Convention, recently signed by the two countries, the captain of the *Yamacraw* could only remain in the area and watch.

Meanwhile, Dowling patrolled along the river looking for any suspicious signs. Near the banks of a marsh he saw tracks indicating that a vessel had recently pulled into the high grass. The sheriff and his men followed the trail inland and captured C. H. Myers, who was armed and guarding a cache of whiskey. The liquor was being hauled to the drawbridge on Atlantic Boulevard, where it was being transferred to trucks and carried into Jacksonville.[20]

This also was the year that President Calvin Coolidge asked Congress to help the Treasury Department by having the navy transfer twenty torpedo boat destroyers and two minesweepers to the Coast Guard. In addition, he wanted funds for the Coast Guard to purchase or build 223 cabin cruisers and 100 smaller motor boats. This was done to close Rum Row, a stretch of ocean just beyond the territorial limits, ranging from New Jersey to Montauk Point, Long Island. Rum Row was the rendezvous point for mother ships bringing liquor to the mid-Atlantic urban population.[21]

Merrill-Stevens profited from Prohibition. Many of the Coast Guard cutters frequently were on the company's ways undergoing repairs. Probably many of the rumrunners' boats were converted or overhauled in the same yard. At least once a Coast Guard cutter was assigned to watch the ninety-two–foot yacht *Victory* while it was being overhauled in the Merrill-Stevens yard. The cutter captain had good reason to be suspicious, for the *Victory* had been captured twice before for violating the national Prohibition act.[22]

By 1927 the Coast Guard had succeeded in reducing the flow of liquor from Rum Row and turned its attention to Florida. One Coast Guard official said: "This move means a real liquor war and what I mean is war. . . . The rum runners are organized. They have a fund to provide for the defense of any of their men who are captured. And they have placed a price on the heads of [m]any of our most active coast guardsmen."[23]

The next year, Prohibition agents were tipped off and waited just south of Jacksonville Beach for rumrunners. This time, a vessel flying a British flag steamed close to shore at about three in the morning. When the agents moved against the ship, the bootleggers jumped into a smaller, faster speedboat and fled, leaving the larger vessel with thirty-five thousand dollars in booze behind to be confiscated.[24]

When Charles Perry and six associates were sent to the federal penitentiary in Atlanta in 1929, the Justice Department alleged that it had broken up the largest rum-running ring in Florida. The department charged that Perry, the son of a former sheriff of St. Johns County, had smuggled more than $250,000 in liquor into the state from February to September 1926. The prosecution stated that Perry had vessels lying forty miles off St. Augustine from which his fleet of small, fast speedboats were supplied with liquor to be off-loaded all along the northeast coast of Florida.[25]

The decade of the 1920s saw more than just rum-running affect maritime life in the port of Jacksonville. Trains and automobiles changed the tourist's mode of travel. No longer were travelers using river steamboats to visit the interior. More often, tourists drove their own cars or traveled by train or bus. And trains and trucks became the preferred carrier for most goods. The St. Johns river steamers gradually were crowded out of business.

However, coastal passenger services continued to use the port until the outbreak of World War II, and in the twenties the Clyde Line, later the Clyde-Mallory Line, launched its building program of six new passenger cruise ships. In 1925–26 the new *Cherokee, Mohawk, Seminole,* and *Algonquin* slid off the ways. Each ship was 402 feet long and 54 foot beam, could make 16 knots, and had accommodations for 350 passengers. In 1927 two larger ships, the *Iroquois* and the *Shawnee,* were built. These two were 408 feet long and 62 foot beam, steamed at 20 knots, and could accommodate 600 passengers.[26]

The USS *Constitution,* crossing the St. Johns Bar at the break of day on 16 December 1931, might be used to signify the change of the decades. Prohibition was nearing an end, economic depression was sweeping the country, and in faraway lands the forces that would shape World War II were gathering force. But to the people of Jacksonville, the arrival of "Old Ironsides" was an opportunity to see and visit the historic beginnings of the nation's maritime might.

In 1905, when it had been recommended that the great lady be used as a target ship, there had been a tremendous outcry throughout the country to save her. In 1906 Congress appropriated $100,000 to rebuild her as much like the original as possible. Then she was anchored in Boston as a naval museum. Again in 1925 the Navy was authorized to restore and equip her as before.

Then, when the work was completed in 1931, it was decided that she should go down the east coast, visiting ports to let the people see the USS *Constitution*. The navy minesweeper *Grebe* towed "Old Ironsides" on her restoration cruise.

When the two vessels rounded Commodores Point at 10:30 A.M., all ships in port let loose with their whistles. The crowds on shore cheered. The *Constitution* was to berth at Williamson Tie Company's dock near the Main Street bridge, until it was discovered that her draft of twenty-two feet was two feet too deep. The problem was solved by placing two lighters between the dock and the ship, and the Jacksonville tug *Three Friends* had the honor of nudging the *Constitution* to the dock. The *Constitution*'s captain, Commander Louis J. Gulliver, greeted Mayor John T. Alsop, Jr., and the Chamber of Commerce representatives, James T. Daniels and Sumter L. Lowry, on the quarterdeck. The public was invited to visit the old man-of-war during the three days of its visit, and hundreds availed themselves of the opportunity.[27]

In 1935 George Reddig began organizing the dock laborers on the Talleyrand Avenue docks. There had been previous attempts to unionize, but they had met with failure. Reddig gathered eleven men to his cause. Shipping executives had never been friendly to organized labor and they did their best to break this attempt, as they had in the past, by blacklisting any known troublemaker. Even other dock workers, fearing that their own jobs might be in jeopardy, were against Reddig.

George Reddig passed out union buttons to his small band of followers, buttons they were afraid to wear openly. However, the twelve were persistent in their efforts to unionize. In 1936 a charter was granted by the International Longshoremen's Association and Reddig became the first president of Local 1408. This legalization of the group led to the open wearing of union buttons and recruiting of members. Within a few years Local 1408 controlled all longshoremen's work on the Talleyrand docks, and the first union benefit was a pay raise from thirty cents an hour to thirty-five cents. More importantly, the workers now had a voice in their working conditions.[28]

Maritime activity was in the doldrums during most of the 1930s, until Hitler invaded Poland in 1939. Then American shipyards received orders to recondition ships for the embattled western European nations. The U.S. Navy began reevaluating its needs, and domestic orders also reached the shipyards. Merrill-Stevens began expanding its facilities and laid plans for a new and larger dry dock.

When the U.S. Navy became interested in developing PT (Patrol Torpedo) boats, Jacksonville's Huckins Yacht Corporation submitted a bid. The navy, desiring to test and standardize PT boats, set up a 190-mile endurance course to evaluate the various models proposed by Elco Corporation of New Jersey, Higgins Yacht Corporation of New Orleans, and Huckins Yacht Corporation. The series of tests became known as the Plywood Derbies. The first evaluation was held in July 1941, over a 190-mile course, running at full throttle from Sarah Ledge, off New London, Connecticut, around the eastern end of Block Island, to *Fire Island Lightship*, with the finish line at Montauk Point Whistling Buoy, off the east end of Long Island.

Four of the PT boats participating failed to complete the course. Elco boats finished first and second with speeds of 39.72 and 37 knots, respectively. The Huckins boat came in third at 33.83 knots. The Higgins PT came in fourth with 31.40 knots. In an earlier trial, Elco had covered a measured mile at 45.3 knots light and 44.1 knots heavy. The Huckins boat was the only other entry to exceed 40 knots, and its speeds were 43.8 knots light and 41.5 knots heavy. In the turning maneuverability test, Huckins PT-69 came in first.

The Navy standardized its PT boats to seventy-five to eighty-two feet in length, to carry three Packard engines, to be able to maintain forty knots for one hour, and to have a cruising radius of five hundred miles. The three companies submitted bids for the thirty-two boats the navy wanted. Higgins was awarded a contract for twenty-four boats and Huckins received a contract for eight. As soon as the United States entered the war, additional PT boats were ordered, with Elco contracted for thirty-six and Huckins for ten more boats.[29]

The Merrill-Stevens new twelve-thousand-ton dry dock was built at a plant on the old Cummer Mill site by the George D. Auchter Company at a cost of a million dollars. It was the largest dry dock in the South, with 556 feet by 95 feet inside the wings. This provided the company with three ways to lift a ship into dry dock. The new facility could bring an oceangoing ship from wet to dry in less than thirty-three minutes. Another method employed the marine railway, with tracks going down to the river bottom. A carriage would roll down, the ship centered upon the apparatus, and the carriage hauled out of the water with the ship secured to its top. In the third method, a platform between two piers would be submerged and the craft placed above it. The platform then would be raised, similar to an elevator, bringing the craft out of water. This last method was designed for smaller vessels.[30]

On 18 February 1943, the Merrill-Stevens new dry dock lifted its first ship, the *Benjamin Franklin*, a liberty ship. The day before, the Gibbs Gas Engine of Florida shipyard launched three vessels, the Patrol Craft PC-615, and two minesweepers, YMS-348 and YMS-349. The port of Jacksonville actively built and repaired ships for the war effort.[31]

The Gibbs shipyard also converted some of the local shrimp boats into navy patrol craft (YP). Some of these YPs were given to the Soviet Union under the Lend Lease Program. Russian naval officers and sailors came to the Mayport naval basin to be trained to operate these YPs. There is an interesting U.S. Navy official photograph, taken at Mayport on 22 October 1944, of the last group of Russian navymen standing with their U.S. Navy instructors. In the background are the YPs, with the Soviet naval ensign clearly visible on the fantail of one of the vessels.[32]

Unknown to most people at the time, Nazi submarines may have mined the approaches to the jetties. Although the government made no acknowledgment of these actions, rumors abound that mines had been laid. Some fishing craft were said to have nearly hit some of the mines, and one mine was supposed to have broken loose and exploded among the rocks at the mouth of the jetties. For a period of several days in the fall of 1942, the U.S. Navy closed some East Coast ports, including Jacksonville. It was June 1945 before the Navy acknowledged that Jacksonville's port had been closed while it looked for enemy mines off the jetties. Oddly, the release did not state that any mines were found, but the following year Captain C. R. Bailey, U.S. Army Air Corps, lecturing at the Army Air Force Special Staff School, stated that ten mines were found off the jetties on 30 September 1942. And there is a photograph in the Mayport Naval Station archives of the navigation chart of the St. Johns jetties with the mine locations drawn in. The mines were almost south of the St. Johns buoy.[33]

But what happened to the Clyde Line's fleet of coastwise passenger ships built in the mid-1920s? The *Mohawk* sank off the New Jersey coast in January 1935, long before the war. The *Iroquois* was acquired by the U.S. Navy in 1940. She was refitted as a hospital ship and renamed the USS *Solace* AH-5. After the war, in 1948, she was sold to Turkey, and returned to being a passenger cruise ship. The War Shipping Administration acquired the *Shawnee* in December 1941, and converted her to a troop transport. After the war she sailed first under a Panamanian registry and then a Yugoslav registry. She was destroyed in a shipyard fire in September 1949. The *Cherokee* became a troopship in January 1942, and six months later, on a return trip, was hit and sunk by two enemy torpedoes. The *Seminole* and the *Algonquin* both were converted to troopships in 1942, and then refitted as hospital ships in 1943. After the war both were laid up in the James River in Virginia. The first was sold for scrap in 1952 and the second followed suit in 1957.[34]

In 1946 the U.S. Navy presented James C. Merrill, president of Merrill-Stevens, a citation for "sending back to sea during the war more than 1,000 repaired or converted ships [for which his company] has earned the Navy's Certificate of Achievement."[35] Thus the two bellwethers, Merrill-Stevens and the Clyde Line, provide a microcosm of legitimate port business in Jacksonville during the first half of the twentieth century. It would be pleasant to think that the bootlegging activities of the port were an aberration. But illegal slave trading in the early 1800s, blockade-running during the Civil War, and filibustering prior to the Spanish-American War established patterns of activities quite in keeping with rum-running.

Chapter Fifteen

THE CONTAINER REVOLUTION AND THE JPA

Jacksonville port activities, like the activities at all ports, are multifaceted: there are municipal and private docks and terminals, shipyards and repair facilities, import and export services, dry and liquid cargos, and a multitude of dock handling methods ranging from stevedore gangs to complicated automated facilities. Not all of these activities operate on the same business cycle, but they do impinge upon each other. If one is ailing for an excessive period of time, the malaise probably will be felt by the other phases of port business. The lack of funds and a municipal port organization became Jacksonville's basic malaise just prior to and after World War II. It took the container revolution and the creation of the Jacksonville Port Authority to correct the situation.

Municipal development of port facilities began in 1912, when a special act of the Floridae legislature authorized the city to buy waterfront property upon which to build docks and terminals. Jacksonville built two piers in 1916 and a third pier in 1925, with a total expenditure of just over three million dollars.

In mid-1945 consulting engineers completed a port and industrial survey which brought to light some serious economic weaknesses. From 1929 to 1936, tonnage over the city's docks and terminals grew each year, including the Depression years. By 1936 traffic was three times the 1929 tonnage. Yet from 1937 to

1939, traffic dropped to 44% of 1936's tonnage. The consultants concluded that the drop was due to the abolition, in 1937, of the port bureau charged with solicitations and advertising. The report placed great emphasis upon selling the facilities of the port.

The statistics for port's wartime operations were equally grim. The consultants found that the municipal docks and terminals were used for loading lend-lease cargo. In 1945 the pattern shifted to a substantial volume of inbound cargo being discharged at dockside. The shippers encountered poor physical conditions, deficient handling equipment, labor shortages, and high handling costs. Collectively these deficiencies caused the War Shipping Administration to allocate a minimum of ships to the municipal docks and terminals.

Administrative control of the municipal docks and terminals was parceled out to three different units. A Board of Pilot Commissioners (appointed by the governor), a harbor master, and the city commission. The consultants felt that the Commissioner of Public Utilities, assigned to supervise the port, could devote only a fraction of his time to the docks and terminals. They recommended that Jacksonville consider a port authority organization for its municipal docks and terminals. However, it was a number of years before this recommendation was acted upon.[1]

On the private side, Eric Rath's TMT Trailer Ferry, Inc., made a positive impact upon Jacksonville's port. In August 1953, TMT shipped its first trailer load of fifty-five hundred pounds from Port Everglades to Puerto Rico. It was the beginning of a new concept in shipping. Rath first thought of using a railroad car ferry to Puerto Rico, but the commonwealth had a narrow-gauge rail system. Then he decided to use highway trailers to deliver the goods. Originally he used deck space on a cement bulk carrier to ship from one to five trailers. The wheels and landing gear were removed before the trailer body was hoisted onto the motorship *Ponce*.

Later Rath experimented with oceangoing barges. He converted and placed two former LSTs (Landing Ship Tank) in service. These carried fifty-five trailers and twenty automobiles on three decks. Seagoing tugs from Moran Towing and Transportation Company towed the LSTs to Puerto Rico. In 1955 the TMT *Puerto Rico*, at one time within sixty-five miles of Hurricane Ione, proved its seaworthiness by crossing without any cargo damage.

By 1956 TMT carried about eight million pounds per month. It had five barges operating to Puerto Rico, and over three hundred motor vehicles carrying goods to the barges. Sixty-five percent of TMT's cargo arrived at the drive-in doors of its barges in company trucks, as Rath sought to coordinate his cargo arrivals to avoid week-long pier delays due to shipping schedules.[2]

That year TMT began its long-term association with Jacksonville, and it decided to use self-propelled trailer ships. It purchased an LSM (Landing Ship Medium) and sent it to the Merrill-Stevens yard for conversion. The TMT *Carib Queen*, 475 feet long with a 72-foot beam, could carry 100 trailers and 100 autos, and had passenger accommodations in five double and two single cabins.

TMT also had Merrill-Stevens build its "sea-truck" to expand service to the smaller islands. This short boxy vessel had a high-top shoe profile, except that the heel was the bow and the toe the stern. The TMT *Seatruck Lloyd* was 64.5 feet long, had a 31-foot beam, and a draft of 6 feet. She could carry four trailers, or nine dispatch vans, or eighteen automobiles, and had a speed of twelve knots. She sailed with a three-man crew.

TMT's Jacksonville terminal was built around the old slips of the Locarno yard on the southside. The bow ramp of the old LSTs let down to a ferry-type ramp. Amidships the company built an earth-fill incline and a ferry ramp. Thus the trailer ships could be loaded simultaneous from the bow and the inclined ramp. According to Rath, this allowed his company to load or unload fifty-five trailers and twenty autos in an eight-hour shift. That same cargo in a standard ship would take three days.[3]

Another pioneer of marine containerization moved to Jacksonville in 1959, when the Sea-Land Service, Inc., opened its terminal on an old pier that later became part of JPA's Talleyrand

Docks & Terminals. According to Sea-Land, this was "just three years after the *Ideal* X ushered in the container age when it lifted the first box from the Port of Houston." Initially Sea-Land shipped an average of sixty-five containers a week to Puerto Rico.[4]

TMT's trailer concept swept through the maritime world. There was much talk that the roll on/roll off (Ro/Ro) approach was a wave of the future. However, some shippers noted a serious weakness in the vast amount of non-paying air space between the deck and the underside of the trailers. Another concept developed utilizing the lift on/lift off (Lo/Lo) principle, which called for lifting the trailer box from the trailer truck and loading only the box aboard ship. Today these two forms of containerization continue to be refined and developed. Through its connections with TMT and Sea-Land Corp., the port of Jacksonville initially was on the leading edge of the container revolution.[5]

A new economic benefit came to the port from an unexpected source when two local stevedoring companies, Strachan Shipping Co. and McGiffin & Co., Inc., set out to lure the automobile trade to Jacksonville. John "Jack" McGiffin talked about the early days after World War II, when cars arrived in small lots:

I remember the first shipment was just seven cars, sometime in 1957. When VW of America announced they were going to bring in 1,000 cars at a time and maintain a stock of 3,000 cars here in the late 50s, we moved our operations from our own terminal to the Talleyrand docks. We always thought car importing would be good for Jacksonville, but no one ever thought it would become as big as it has.[6]

Meanwhile, due to the lack of proper funding and the neglect of the city commission, the municipal docks and piers were literally falling into the St. Johns River. The finger piers, with warehouses out on the ends, were designed to berth ships on each side, but they had deteriorated so badly that only a portion of one pier could be used. Influential businessmen, and the Chamber of Commerce, demanded that the port be taken from city government and run as a business. State Senator John Mathews developed these ideas into a legislative proposal which he presented to the Florida legislature.

In 1963 the Jacksonville Port Authority, an independent agency, was empowered to operate the port facilities in Duval County. The city had to transfer its municipal docks and terminals, including the dock and terminal railroad, over to the JPA; Duval County had to turn over Blount Island, that underdeveloped spoil area in the St. Johns River created when the Corps of Engineers dredged the Fulton Cutoff. In return, the JPA had to pay the city $1.5 million for the docks and terminal. Blount Island changed hands gratis.[7]

Other symbolic occurrences happened in 1963. When the city built its waterfront parking lot next to City Hall, inspection of the dilapidated riverfront yielded the sunken hull of the Clyde Line's river steamer *Osceola*. The 250-foot-long steamer had been active until 1928. Then she had been tied up along an unused section of the waterfront. Over the years she settled on the bottom. In 1937 her topsides had been dismantled, and, as the hull sank into the mud, she was forgotten. The cutting and removing of the mud-filled hull brought one of the last vestiges of the River Steamboat Era to an end. Jacksonville turned to the sea.[8]

Other links to the past dropped from the scene when the Merrill-Stevens Dry Dock and Repair, the Rawls Brothers Shipyard, and the St. Johns Division were merged to create a new facility—the Jacksonville Shipyard Inc., with Martin E. Kirwin as president.[9]

Initially the JPA had the power to direct the city commission to levy a tax of 1.5 mills and to borrow $200,000 to begin its operations. Unfortunately for the JPA, the authority to levy a tax was soon withdrawn, and in its place the city provided $800,000 annually. Dave Rawls, the first managing director of the JPA, knew that financing was a top priority. In 1968, he set out to raise $25 million through a bond issue, which was successful.

But Rawls did not neglect the physical plant. Earlier, in 1965, using the initial money, he built marginal wharves to which Sea-Land Service Inc. moved. This was the first facility placed in operation and the start of the rebuilding of the municipal port. Later, with the money from the bond issue, further expansion took place and JPA developed its facilities to handle auto imports. [10]

The next two managing directors, Robert C. Peace (1970–1973) and James Scott, Jr. (1973–1978) continued port development. However, much of their time was taken up with the Offshore Power Systems's attempt to build floating nuclear power plants in the port. It began on 8 March 1972, when Westinghouse Electric Co. and Tenneco Corp. announced that the two were joining forces to build these plants, and that Jacksonville was among the ports being considered to site this venture.

By the time the Tenneco directors met in Houston on 14 April, the site selection had been narrowed to 900 acres of Blount Island in Jacksonville or 750 acres in Portsmouth, Virginia. Mayor Hans Tanzler had the nearly unanimous backing of the business and civic leaders of the community in his attempt to bring OPS to Jacksonville. By 1 May 1972, the Jacksonville Port Authority had sold the 900-acre parcel of undeveloped land to OPS for $2,000 an acre. Four days later the city council approved OPS's dredge-and-fill permits for Back River to create the site for its manufacturing plant. Three weeks later the Florida Cabinet approved the permits, and two days after that Westinghouse-Tenneco selected Jacksonville. Mayor Tanzler called the decision "Jacksonville's finest hour."[11]

Westinghouse-Tenneco claimed that 42 percent of the electrical energy generated in the United States lay within two hundred miles of the Atlantic, Gulf, or Pacific coasts. Floating generating plants would provide many additional sites close to the country's load centers. [12] Also there were savings inherent in their venture, for construction would take place in a new shipyard facility employing nautical assembly-line concepts.

OPS intended to dredge Back River to create a slip around which the company's manufacturing plants would be based. The floating platforms would be built at the inland end of the slip.

The platform would journey outboard along the slip. At each production area the next component part of the plant would be completed. The slip was to be a 530-foot square within which the 400-foot square floating platforms would be built. The slip was the central feature of OPS's manufacturing facility.[13]

OPS also ordered a huge gantry crane from Krupp Industries in Germany. The crane had a span of 675 feet, and the bottom of its 50-foot–high girder beam was 300 feet above the ground. It arrived in Jacksonville on 4 May 1975, and was assembled on the site early in 1976.[14]

In the summer of 1974 Harry Shorstein, recently appointed the city's general counsel, wrote an unfavorable legal opinion on the proposed contract between the Jacksonville Electric Authority and OPS. Shorstein maintained that the contract would either bankrupt the city or place it at the mercy of OPS. Soon Jacksonville's business and political communities were split over this opinion.

Public Service Electric & Gas of New Jersey, which had ordered four plants, asked OPS to delay the delivery date for five years; then, late in 1974, the Jacksonville Electric Authority let its letter of intent expire. These actions caused OPS to slow its construction plans, for it could not expend such sums without an adequate backlog of orders. Four years later, Public Service Electric & Gas canceled its orders.[15] During all of this time, the managing director of the JPA was intimately involved in this port development.

Ironically, in December 1981, the Nuclear Regulatory Commission told OPS that it would soon receive licenses to build its plants. But by that time the company had no customers, nor any prospects, for the Three Mile Island incident of 1979 had effectively dried up the demand for nuclear generating plants.

On 17 February 1982, OPS accepted defeat and said that it would phase out its remaining operations in Jacksonville by September of that year. One of its final gestures to the city was to sell a hundred acres of its holdings on Blount Island back to the city at its purchase price of two thousand dollars per acre.[16]

A more serious setback for the JPA took place back in 1975 when the city council stopped providing the $800,000 funding for port development. The cessation of funding continued for eleven years. Once again, port construction entered the doldrums.

When John "Jack" Mackroth became managing director (1978–1984), he changed the direction of the agency. He felt that the JPA should be a leasing agency rather than an operating agency. Following Mackroth's lead, the JPA now leases about 75 percent of its facilities. In 1984, when Mackroth retired, his successor, Paul D. deMariano, took over in the midst of a series of economic squalls. James R. Hagy, writing in the *Florida Trend,* summarized the situation: "When Paul deMariano took charge of the Jacksonville Port Authority four years ago, the agency's seaport was withering. It was overly dependent on automobile imports, a trade that, ironically, had built the port. It lacked adequate public funding for expansion, and its facilities were far inferior to rival ports in Charleston, South Carolina, and Savannah and Brunswick, Georgia. While these ports built facilities for containerized cargo and bought huge container cranes, the Port of Jacksonville paved more land for auto imports."[17]

Two years after deMariano arrived, Jacksonville voters rejected a referendum which would have allowed JPA funding through tax money. During the following year and a half, BMW of America, Hyundai, Peugeot, Saab, and Volkswagen, claiming industrial pollution fallout had damaged their cars' finishes on the municipal docks, left Jacksonville for Brunswick, Georgia.

DeMariano met his problems head on, and, by creating an aggressive marketing program, began selling the port of Jacksonville. Although he probably knew nothing of the 1945 survey, he was following its conclusions.

To overcome the loss of funding, the new director turned to issuing JPA marine revenue bonds. And for the auto trade, deMariano organized JPA's first Auto Importers Appreciation Day, with golfing, tennis, and a cruise on the St. Johns River. DeMariano's appreciation went further: he increased the foreign trade zone on Blount Island from 5 to 119 acres. Foreign trade zones are considered beyond United States customs territory. Thus auto importers could store more cars on duty-free land and defer customs payments to a future date. This was a positive way to entice auto importers, for it improved their cash flow position. Since then, Diahatsu America, Inc., has selected Jacksonville for its southeast import center. [18]

According to JPA's Director of Trade Development Neal Ganzel, Jr., the container revolution is now moving into the third wave of its development. First came the creation of containers, special cranes, and container ships. Second came the building of marine terminals to service these new container ships. The third wave is creating intermodal connections. This means that the terminals must have easy, ready access to other modes of transportation to speed the container on to its ultimate destination, preferably with as little handling as possible between the originator and the consumer.

It is this third wave which is the linchpin of Director deMariano's marketing approach in his search for new business. Jacksonville is serviced by three railroads, ten or twelve of the nation's top trucking companies, and two interstate highways less than an hour from the docks and terminals. But all of these intermodal connections would be meaningless if Jacksonville, in terms of mileage, were not midway between the Southeast's major metropolitan areas of Atlanta and Miami. Demographically Jacksonville has thirty-three million consumers within a ten-hour drive. [19]

COSMOS is a significant part of the JPA's intermodal connection. One dictionary definition of cosmos is "an orderly harmonious systematic universe." JPA's COSMOS or "Computerized On-line Service for Marine Operational System" is a $1.4 million computer system designed to create "an orderly harmonious systematic universe" between JPA, its customers, and the U.S. Customs Service. The hardware for this system was installed in April 1987, and the software modules are being phased in gradually. [20]

DeMariano's marketing approach began to pay off. In mid-1987 American Transport Lines, a Crowley Maritime Corp. subsidiary, moved to JPA's facilities from its private terminal in Jacksonville. The company considered moving to Charleston or Savannah, but deMariano suggested staying in Jacksonville and moving to the Talleyrand docks. Arno Dimmling, Crowley's vice president of terminals, said the company decided to stay because of its "capital commitment there and deMariano's willingness to accommodate Crowley. 'Paul is one of the best marketeers I've run into in the port business. . . . We required special facilities that didn't exist, namely container cranes at Talleyrand. He was willing to move the cranes we needed from Blount Island to Talleyrand on the basis of our commitment to moving.' "[21]

In February 1988, JPA and Sea-Land agreed to a major expansion of the carrier's business in Jacksonville. Sea-Land will move from JPA's Talleyrand docks to Blount Island, and JPA will spend about forty million dollars to develop the facilities for Sea-Land's containerization complex. In return, the carrier will share space aboard its Atlantic-class ships with P&O Containers Ltd. and Nedlloyd Lijnen B. V. In essence, Sea-Land is designating JPA's Blount Island as one of its load centers for its South Atlantic/Gulf route to northern Europe, and bringing new shippers to the port.[22]

Meanwhile, it appeared that the JPA was neglecting the bulk cargo aspect of its terminals. The 1989 fiscal year, which ended 30 September, had a 66-percent drop in dry bulk tonnage from fiscal 1988. However, just over a month into fiscal 1990, JPA announced that Dravo Basic Materials Inc. will lease six acres on Blount Island and begin bringing rock aggregate into the port. The first year will bring two hundred thousand tons and it is expected that the total could reach five to six hundred thousand tons at the end of five years.[23]

DeMariano's marketing exploits brought corresponding labor changes to JPA's docks. In 1987 deMariano replaced ILA's warehouse workers with lower-paid JPA workers. When the ILA went on strike, the Duval County Circuit Court ruled that both union and non-union workers could be employed in JPA's warehouses. Many considered this ruling to apply to the docks as well. Later, when American Transport Lines brought its Teamsters Union workers to the JPA docks, President Charles F. Spencer of ILA #1408 decided not to challenge this intrusion into what had formally been the exclusive domain of his union. On 18 March 1987, the stevedore company of Green Cove Maritime, Inc., unloaded the first ship at JPA docks with non-union workers.[24]

Charles Spencer, knowing that Florida is a right-to-work state, has accepted the challenge to his union. He, too, is resorting to marketing his product—a highly trained, skilled, well-motivated longshoreman who gets the work done efficiently and profitably. And he can point with pride to the fact that even JPA officials credit his union with keeping many of the automobile imports coming to the port of Jacksonville "because of the low vehicle damage rate on local docks." But for the future, he knows that his union must demonstrate daily to the port's shippers the old adage that "you get what you pay for," and that the extra pay for his longshoremen reaps rewards for the shipper.[25]

In July 1989 Jacksonville Shipyards, Inc., was sold to Terex Corporation of Green Bay, Wisconsin. This is the first venture of Terex, a manufacturer of heavy equipment, into the shipyard business. Then, on 9 November 1989, Terex announced that, unless there were a buyer for the shipyard soon, the company would shut down the downtown yards on 8 January 1990. Actually JSI consists of three separate divisions. The Mayport Naval Station Division and the Bellinger Division were not included in the shutdown. The downtown shipyards closed in January 1990.[26]

By August Terex reopened its downtown yards and sought business, after the union workers agreed to a new contract wherein they could be assigned to several different jobs. The company also agreed that it was top-heavy in management and slashed a number of positions in the upper echelons. With these changes,

JSI reopened. On 28 August 1990, the TMT barge *Jacksonville* was towed in, and 100 laborers returned to work on the 730-foot, 3 level barge.[27]

The dismantlement of OPS's giant crane began in 1990. In 1985 Gate Maritime Properties, Inc., purchased all of OPS's Blount Island holdings. Westinghouse had paid about $15.5 million for the crane; Gate bought the crane and 780 acres of land for $16.7 million. Gate, in turn, entered into negotiations with the People's Republic of China for the crane. When the deal was completed, workers assembled to take down the huge gantry crane.[28]

As the crane came down, a new bridge across the St. Johns, just upriver from Blount Island, opened. The Dames Point bridge will bring new multi-lane highways to the north shore of Blount Island, further increasing the accessibility of the area. This led to the opening of construction for a four-lane bridge to Blount Island. Prior to this, Blount Island, close to the mouth of the river, had ready access to the sea but limited access to land transportation. All of this is now changing.[29]

More significant than these physical changes taking place is the leadership change in the JPA. Managing director Paul deMariano stepped down on 1 July 1990. C. Cliff Mendoza became the acting and then the permanent managing director.

The deMariano tenure brought growth to the JPA. From 1983 to 1989, port revenues rose from $12 to $17 million while assets increased from $104 to $156 million. But expenses moved from $5.8 to $12.8 million, and the long-term debt went from $36.8 to $83.4 million. DeMariano tried to get the state legislature to provide some of the funding and failed. He met the same result from the people of Duval County with a request for a property tax increase. Finally, he turned to issuing revenue bonds for his facilities improvements. In deMariano's words: "We've taken on a lot of debt. We're maxed out."[30] Apparently, deMariano believes that the excitement of dynamic growth ended when the JPA became "maxed out," and it was time to move on.

The next month, before deMariano's departure could be evaluated, United States forces were deployed to the Persian Gulf under Operation Desert Shield. Just four days after the president ordered the deployment, the first ship of the Military Sealift Command left the Blount Island terminal for the Middle East. In the first three months, thirty-three ships were sent from Jacksonville. Colonel Richard G. Simmons of the 1181st Army Transportation Unit said that Jacksonville and Houston were the two major ports sending supplies to the deployed troops.[31]

In addition to the merchant ships, combatant ships from Mayport Naval Station immediately responded to Desert Shield. The aircraft carrier *Saratoga* and four of its escorts already were in the Mediterranean Sea, and, although not a part of the *Saratoga's* battle group, the Mayport-based minesweeper *Impervious* also operated in the Middle East. The port of Jacksonville was closely bound to Desert Shield.[32]

Cliff Mendoza, more financially restrained than his predecessor, is trying to develop financing to continue modernizing the port. Late in October he met with officials of the Crowley Maritime Corporation to discuss a hundred-acre terminal on Blount Island to allow the company to consolidate its terminals in one area. To do this, Mendoza mentioned the need to acquire new land, perhaps at Dames Point, to house JPA's auto facilities. This would accommodate both parties. To finance such a move, Mendoza suggested a new approach wherein some form of public/private joint venture might be developed.[33]

Today there are thirty-four terminals and facilities along the twenty-five mile stretch from downtown Jacksonville to the sea. It might be appropriate to summarize the activities of the larger installations. The Jacksonville Shipyards Inc. and the North Florida Shipyards are the farthest upriver. Jacksonville Shipyards is in downtown Jacksonville just downriver from the Main Street bridge, and North Florida Shipyards is next to it on Commodores Point.

Just upriver from JPA docks, TMT, now a subsidiary of Crowley Maritime Corporation, has new trailer barges which are six hundred feet long with their three decks rising higher than a five-story building. TMT's tri-level loading tower loads all three decks simultaneously by the Ro/Ro method. The barges, with a capacity of 514 trailers, are towed by nine-thousand-horsepower seagoing tugs.

Downriver from the JPA are a number of fuel depots. The Jacksonville Bulk Terminals is located in a small inlet in the midst of these fuel depots. The parent company is Occidental Chemical Company, and for over twenty years Jacksonville Bulk Terminals has shipped superphosphoric acid to the Soviet Union.

Farther downriver, where the Trout River joins the St. Johns, is the Eastern Seaboard Petroleum Company, an independent oil company. All told, there are nine oil terminals in the port, representing the major oil companies and the U.S. Navy Fuel Depot. Eastern Seaboard Petroleum, with twenty-two oil tanks, has the largest oil storage capacity in Jacksonville.

Next to Eastern Seaboard is the U.S. Gypsum Company. The company located in Jacksonville in 1938 to be close to its Southern markets. Presently Florida ranks just behind California as a consumer of wallboard. U.S. Gypsum ships tons of gypsum rock from the company's Nova Scotia quarry to Jacksonville, where it is made into wallboard.[34]

Continuing downriver, beyond Blount Island and at the juncture of the Intracoastal Waterway and the St. Johns, is the Atlantic Marine, Inc. and its affiliate, Atlantic Dry Dock. Atlantic Marine constructs vessels up to 250 feet. It uses an inverted hull method wherein the fabrication of the hull is done upside down so as to produce better welds. Atlantic Dry Dock can handle ships up to 450 feet in length, and has overhauled many of the U.S. Navy's smaller combatant ships from the Mayport Carrier Basin.[35]

In spite of the numerous and varied maritime activities at Jacksonville's port, there is only one organization equipped to actively seek new port business, the JPA. Yet it is a difficult task for the JPA to perform in light of recent financial rebuffs and lack of community recognition. Still, the JPA's role is vital if the port is to live up to its potential.

Notes

Chapter 1: French Rivals

1. Parry and Sherlock, *Short History*, 35–37.
2. Snodgrass, "A River of Many Names," 1.
3. Bennett, *Three Voyages*, 50.
4. Tebeau, *History of Florida*, 29–34.
5. Lyon, "Forts Caroline and San Mateo," 9, 45.
6. Tebeau, *History of Florida*, 29–42; Waterbury, *The Oldest City*, 27–40.

Chapter 2: The English Challenge

1. Crane, *Southern Frontier*, 3, 9.
2. Fleetwood, *Tidecraft*, 29–32.
3. Crane, *Southern Frontier*, 75–77; TePaske, *Governorship*, 110.
4. Crane, *Southern Frontier*, 79–80.
5. Ibid., 81.
6. TePaske, *Governorship*, 131.
7. Ibid., 140–44.
8. Ibid., 150–51.

Chapter 3: The False Dawn

1. Cabell and Hanna, *St. Johns*, 93.
2. Ward, *Old Hickory's Town*, 64.
3. Martin Jollie to Tonyn, 13 February 1776, Great Britain Public Records Office, Colonial Office, CO 5/556, duplicate 39 (hereinafter cited as CO).
4. Clark, *Naval Documents*, 4: 225, 702–3, 825.
5. Ibid., 5: 328; Siebert, *Loyalists*, 1: 39; Arana, "Calendar" [part 1], 41–43.
6. Arana, "Calendar" [part 2], 71–78; Siebert, *Loyalists*, 1: 39–40.
7. Arana, "Calendar" [part 2], 71–72, 74–75.
8. Smith, "Mermaids Riding Alligators," 450.

9. Clark, *Naval Documents*, 6: 313–14, 717, 1468; Siebert, *Loyalists*, 1: 44.

10. Tonyn to Prevost, 17 January 1777, CO 5/557: 278.

11. Tonyn to Germaine, 2 April 1777, CO 5/557: 262, 5 May 1777, CO 5/557: 405–06; Pennington, "East Florida," 32.

12. Siebert, *Loyalists*, 1: 46–47; Tonyn to Germaine, 16 June 1777, CO 5/557: 481–82; Bennett, *Southernmost*, 6; Ward, *Hickory's Town*, 76–78.

13. Bennett, *Southernmost*, 16.

14. Ibid., 16–17.

15. Tonyn to Prevost, CO 5/558: 35–36.

16. Jordan to Tonyn, 6 March 1778, CO 5/558: 255–56; Tonyn to Germaine, 20 March 1778, CO 5/558: 226–27.

17. Butler, *Annals*, 1: 303, appendix 2; Siebert, *Loyalists*, 1: 56; Tonyn to Germaine, 28 April 1778, CO 5/558: 251–53.

18. Tonyn to Germaine, 28 April 1778, CO 5/558: 251–53; Ibid., 15 March 1778, CO 5/558: 314; Mowat, *East Florida*, 114.

19. Bennett, *Southernmost*, 35.

20. Tonyn to Germaine, 3 July 1778, CO 5/558: 375; Butler, *Annals*, 1: 311, appendix 2.

21. Tonyn to Germaine, 24 July 1778, CO5/558: 412–14.

22. Pennington, "East Florida," 45.

23. Siebert, *Loyalists*, 1: 117–18, 177.

Chapter 4: One More Time

1. Parker, "Canoes," 57.

2. Cabell and Hanna, *St Johns*, 139–40.

3. Hanna and Hanna, *Golden Sands*, 57.

4. Ibid., 61–62; Ward, *Hickory's Town*, 89–94.

5. Hanna and Hanna, *Golden Sands*, 99–100; May, "Kingsley," 147, 154.

6. Cabell and Hanna, *St. Johns*, 162–63; Benjamin, "The Sea Islands," 845.

7. May, "Kingsley," 149, 151.

8. Patrick, *Florida Fiasco*, 17, 46.

9. Ibid., 166.

10. Ibid., 102.

11. Ibid., 182.

12. Ibid., 185.

13. May, "Kingsley," 151.

14. Ibid.

15. *Niles' Weekly Register*, 3: 154, 311–12, 4: 159.

Chapter 5: Frontier Engineers

1. [Simmons], *Notices*, 24–26.

2. Clarence E. Carter, *Papers*, 23: 476–77, 755–56, 816, 835–37, 846–47, 854–55; 24: 77–80; U.S. Congress, H. Doc. 61/23/1, 61–65.

3. Clarence E. Carter, *Papers*, 24: 79–80.

4. *Dictionary of American Biography*, s.v. "James Gadsden."

5. Clarence E. Carter, *Papers*, 24: 246–48.

6. Ibid., 312–13.

7. Ibid., 426–28.

8. U.S. National Archives, RG 77, D-362 (1829), D-333 (1829), Entry 17, Box 29; Ibid., G-67 (1826), G-181 (1828), Entry 17, Box 44; Ibid., microfilm T-1113, Roll 1, Alexander Macomb to John Grant, 6 November 1826; Ibid., T-1113, Roll 2;, Macomb to Grant, 11 July 1828.

9. Clarence E. Carter, *Papers*, 24: 836–38, 846–47.

10. U.S. National Archives, RG 77, M-1647, M-1663, M-1677 (1836).

11. Sprague, *Origin*, 148.

12. U.S. National Archives, RG 77, M-1695, M-1725, M-1750 (1836); M-1829 (1837).

13. Clarence E. Carter *Papers*, 25: 337–39; H. Doc. 3/25/2, 320.

Chapter 6: Seminoles, Steamers, and a Seaport

1. Clarence A. Carter, *Papers* 22: 477–78.

2. Rahn, *River Highway*, 34; The *Florida News* (Jacksonville), 22 May 1852.

3. Buckman, "Letters," 16–22.

4. U.S. National Archives, RG 24, Logbook, USS *Sparks*.

5. Rahn, *River Highway*, appendix B, 13; Mueller, "Steamboat Activity," 408.

6. Mueller, "Steamboat Activity," 408–09.

7. *American State Papers: Military Affairs*, 7: 811.

8. Williams, *The Territory of Florida*, 248–50.

9. Francke, *Fort Mellon*, 51–52; *Army and Navy Chronicle* (Washington, D.C.), 5: 381.

10. Clarence E. Carter, *Papers*, 26: 279–81, 432.

11. Anderson, *Florida Territory*, 10, 15–16.

12. Davis, *History*, 358–59.

13. Ibid.

14. Baldwin, "St. Johns Bar," 321–27.

15. U.S. Army, Corps of Engineers, *Annual Report*, 1827, 1: 663.

16. Fineren, "Conditions," 19.

17. Baldwin, "St. Johns Bar," 328.

18. Baldwin, "St. Johns Bar," 330.

Chapter 7: The Blockade

1. Martin and Schafer, *Jacksonville's Ordeal*, 40–42.

2. Ibid., 54; Potter and Nimitz, *Sea Power*, 257.

3. Potter and Nimitz, *Sea Power*, 256; U.S. Navy Department, Naval History Division, *Civil War*, VI-256.

4. Martin and Schafer, *Jacksonville's Ordeal*, 54–55.

5. Davis, *History*, 125.

6. U.S. Navy Department, Naval History Division, *Civil War*, I-29, I-37, I-39, II-27.

7. *Official Records* I, 12: 393–95.

8. Ibid., 564, 718–19.

9. U.S. Navy Department, Naval History Division, *Civil War*, I-17, I-27, I-31.

10. Martin and Schafer, *Jacksonville's Ordeal* 58–59.

11. *Official Records*, I, 12: 708–09.

12. Martin and Schafer, *Jacksonville's Ordeal*, 59–60.
13. Ibid.; *Official Records*, I, 12: 573–75.
14. Robinson, "Account," 26–28; *The War of Rebellion*, I, 6: 100; *Florida Sentinel* (Tallahassee), 18 March and 1 April 1862; Johns, *Florida During the Civil War*, 64–66.

Chapter 8: The Inner Blockade

1. Ward, *Old Hickory's Town*, 143; ORN, I, 12: 638–40.
2. When the United States acquired Florida, the old Spanish fort, Castillo de San Marcos, was renamed Fort Marion; East, "St. Augustine During the Civil War," 75–91.
3. Ibid., 645–46; *Official Records*, I, 13: 64–65, 83–84, 86, 90–91, 147; *The War of Rebellion*, I, 6: 111–12; *Florida Sentinel*, 1 April 1862; Ammen, *Old Navy and the New*, 364.
4. *Official Records*, I, 12: 748–50, 804–05.
5. Ibid., 722.
6. Ibid., 13: 90–91, 163–64.
7. Ibid., 163–64.
8. Ibid., 467.
9. *The War of Rebellion*, I, 6: 426–27.
10. Ibid., 53: 233–34.
11. Ibid., 232–33.
12. Ibid., 234–36.
13. Martin and Schafer, *Jacksonville's Ordeal*, 95, 98.
14. *Official Records*, I, 13: 220.
15. Martin and Schafer, *Jacksonville's Ordeal*, 101–03.
16. DuPont and three other flag officers were commissioned rear admirals on 16 July 1862. Hamersly, *A Naval Encyclopaedia*, 22.
17. Martin and Schafer, *Jacksonville's Ordeal*, 104–11.
18. *Official Records*, I, 13: 43.
19. Ibid., 358–59, 362–64, 366–67.
20. Ibid., 245–46.
21. Ibid., 437, 477–78.
22. Ibid., 436, 427–28.
23. Ibid., 461–62.
24. Ibid.
25. Ibid., 463–64.
26. Hayes, *Du Pont*, 319–20; *Official Records*, I, 13: 742, 777.
27. *Official Records*, I, 13: 276–77, 280–81.
28. See "The Battle of Olustee," chapter 12, Johns, *Florida*, for a concise account of and the reasons for this battle.
29. Martin and Schafer, *Jacksonville's Ordeal*, 218–23.
30. *Official Records*, I, 15: 451–53; Dickison, *Dickison*, 65–67.
31. *The War of Rebellion*, I, 35, part 1: 371.
32. Reiger, "Florida After Secession," 139.
33. Dickison, *Dickison*, 73.

Chapter 9: The Steamboat Era

1. Blakey, *Parade*, 115–16.
2. Ibid., 117–19.

3. Ibid., 122.
4. Mueller, *St. Johns*, 7–9.
5. Ibid., 10–11.
6. Ward, *Old Hickory's Town*, 157.
7. Blakey, *Parade*, 124–25.
8. Smiley, *Florida*, 19–20.
9. Cabell and Hanna, *St. Johns*, 180.
10. Mueller, *St. Johns*, 12–14; Blakey, *Parade*, 137.
11. Mueller, *St. Johns*, 12–14.
12. Ibid., 28–29; Craig, "Steamboat Days," 140.
13. Taggart, *Evolution*, 93–95.
14. Mueller, *St. Johns*, 76–81.
15. Ibid., 81.
16. Ibid., 71.
17. Ibid., 70–75, 188, 189.
18. *New York Sun*, 20 September 1896.
19. *Florida Times-Union & Citizen*, 8 February 1897; H. Doc. 37/85/1, 13.
20. S. Doc. 36/54/2, 3.
21. *Florida Times-Union & Citizen*, 8 February 1897.
22. *New York Sun*, 20 September 1896.
23. *Florida Times-Union & Citizen*, 16 January, 18 August 1897.
24. Ibid., 14, 20 September 1897.
25. *Florida Times Union & Citizen*, 10 February, 22 September 1898.
26. U.S. Army, Corps of Engineers, *Annual Report*, 1905, part 2: 1, 318.
27. H. Doc. 37/85/1, 27–28.
28. U.S. Army, Corps of Engineers *Annual Report*, 1933, part 1: 444.
29. Ward, *Old Hickory's Town*, 158, 166, 172.

Chapter 10: Down to the Sea

1. Martin, *The City Makers*, 148.
2. Baldwin, "St. Johns Bar," 333.
3. U.S. Army, Corps of Engineers, *Annual Report*, 1869: 269–72.
4. Ibid., 1872, part 1: 666.
5. Ibid., 1871, part 2: 578–85.
6. Engineers Report Capt. Geo. W. Cullum to W. G. DeSaussure . . . Charleston, S.C., Nov. 20th, 1857, is contained in Bache, *Report*, 56–57; Trenholm, *Report*, 4; U.S. Army, Corps of Engineers, *Annual Report*, 1857, part 2: 221–23; 1872, part 2: 666–72; 1874, part 2: 11–13; 1875, part 2: 37–41; Black, *Hopper Dredging*, 27–28.
7. U.S. Army, Corps of Engineers, *Annual Report*, 1872, part 2: 662–72.
8. Ibid., 1874, part 2: 11.
9. Martin, "Minute Book," 11.
10. Ibid., 51.
11. Martin, *City Makers*, 148.
12. Ibid., 150.
13. Ibid., 149.
14. Rawls, "Ninety-six," 63.
15. Davis, *History*, 387.
16. Rawls, "Ninety-six," 54.

17. Davis, *History*, 388.

18. Rawls, "Ninety-six," 54–55.

19. Ibid., 56.

20. U.S. Army, Corps of Engineers, *Annual Report*, 1883, part 1: 946; 1885, part 2: 1249; 1887, part 2: 1213–14.

21. Rawls, "Ninety-six," 57; Fineren, "Historical."

22. Martin, *City Makers*, 151; Rawls, "Ninety-Six," 57.

23. Davis, *History*, 389.

24. *The Florida Times-Union*, 6, 7, 8, 9 August 1912.

25. Ibid., 16 October 1916.

26. *Jacksonville Seafarer*, February 1982, 4–5; U.S. Army, Corps of Engineers, Water Resources Support Center, *Ports*, 2.

Chapter 11: Filibustering

1. Godoy, "Huau," 196–203; Brown, *Correspondent's*, 69.

2. Godoy, "Huau," 201–02.

3. Ibid., 202.

4. Ibid., 203; Proctor, *Broward*, 100–04, 109–10.

5. Brown, *Correspondent's*, 38–39.

6. Proctor, *Broward*, 114–16.

7. *New York Times*, 20 June 1896.

8. Proctor called the Key West steamer *The City of Key West*; whereas the *New York Times* used that name and *The City of Richmond* interchangeably. Proctor, *Broward*, 116–19; *New York Times*, 27 June 1896.

9. Brown, *Correspondent's*, 65.

10. Proctor, *Broward*, 119.

11. Ibid.

12. John O'Brien, *Captain Unafraid*, 114.

13. Rickenbach, "Filibustering," 230–38.

14. Proctor, *Broward*, 123–28.

15. Rickenbach, "Filibustering," 239–40.

16. Brown, *Correspondent's*, 64–67.

17. Ibid., 67; Proctor, *Broward*, 129–32.

18. Brown, *Correspondent's*, 68.

19. Ibid., 72.

20. Ward, *Old Hickory's Town*, 153–54.

21. Brown, *Correspondent's*, 74–76.

22. Paine, *Roads of Adventure*, 175.

23. Rickenbach, "Filibustering," 242–52.

24. Benton, *International Law*, 43–45.

25. O'Brien, *Captain Unafraid*, 111 –12.

Chapter 12: Coastal Defense: St. Johns Bluff

1. Ex. Doc. 1/14/1, 5–27, passim.

2. Alger, *Spanish-American War*, 38.

3. Bloxham to Long, 27 November & 7 December 1897, Florida State Archives, RG 101, Series 32, vol. 50.

4. Davis, *History*, 208.

5. *Florida Times-Union & Citizen*, 6 March 1898.

6. Ibid., 7 March 1898.

7. Ibid., 14 March 1898.

8. Ibid., 4, 5, 6 April 1898; Wilson to Benyaurd, 2 April 1898, RG 77, Entry 103: 25409, National Archives, Washington, DC (hereafter cited as NA).

9. Albright to Benyaurd, 4, 5 April 1898, RG 77, Atlanta Federal Archives & Record Center, East Point, GA (hereafter cited as EP).

10. Benyaurd to Wilson, 4, 7 April 1898, RG 77, Entry 1163, Box 1, EP; Florida Finance Co to Benyaurd and Sarah F. Williams to Benyaurd, 4 April 1898, RG 77, Entry 103:25409, NA; Browne to Benyaurd, 13 May 1898, RG 77, Entry 1170, Box 1, EP.

11. Benyaurd to Cook and to Einig, 8 April 1898; Benyaurd to Wilson, 12 April 1898, RG 77, Entry 1163, Box 1, EP.

12. Benyaurd to Wilson, 27 May 1898, RG 77, Entry 103:25409, NA; Operations Report for June 1898, RG 77, Entry 1163, Box 1, EP; RG 77, Fortifications File, Drawer 191, Sheet 2, NA.

13. *Florida Times-Union & Citizen*, 22 April 1898.

14. Benyaurd to Wilson, 15 April 1898, RG 77, Entry 1163, Box 1; Benyaurd to Wilson, 14 April 1899, RG 77, Entry 1170, Box 1, EP.

15. Benyaurd to Wilson, 21 April 1898, RG 77, Entry 103:25409, NA; Benyaurd to Smith, 30 April 1898, and Benyaurd to Wilson, 10 May 1898, RG 77, Entry 1163, Box 1, EP.

16. Wilson to Alger and Davis, 20 April 1898, RG 77, Entry 103:25409, NA.

17. *Florida Times-Union & Citizen*, 24 April 1898.

18. Ibid., 22 April 1898.

19. Report of Operations for May 1898, RG 77, Entry 1163, Box 1, EP; RG 77, Fortifications File, Drawer 191, Sheet 2, 4-4, NA.

20. Bliss, *Modern Guns and Mortars*, 140, 143, 155.

21. Report of Operations, June & July, 1898, RG 77, Entry 1163, Box 1, EP; Matloff, *American Military History*, 182.

22. Benyaurd to Wilson, 7 May 1898, RG 77, Entry 1163, Box 1, EP.

23. Navy Department, BuNav to Adj. Gen. Fla., 25 May 1929, Florida State Archives, RG 197, Serial 1207.

24. Benyaurd to Wilson, 7 May, 15 June, 4 Nov. 1898; Benyaurd to Harts, 30 May 1898, RG 77, Entry 1163, Box 1, EP.

25. Benyaurd to Wilson, 30 April 1898, ibid.

26. Benyaurd to Wilson, 10, 11 June 1898, RG 77, Entry 103:27107, NA.

27. Benyaurd to Collector, Port of Jacksonville, 19 August 1898, RG 77, Entry 1163, Box 1, EP.

28. Benyaurd to Wilson, 11 March 1898, RG 77, Entry 103:29220, NA.

29. Benyaurd to Wilson, 24 September 1898; Benyaurd to Cook, 12 November 1898, RG 77, Entry 1163, Box 1, EP.

30. Bliss, *Modern Guns and Mortars*, 173; U.S. Army, Corps of Engineers, *Annual Report*, 1899, 1:889.

31. Merrill to Benyaurd, 21 March 1899, RG 77, Entry 1163, Box 1, EP.

32. Benyaurd to Wilson, 16 February, 11 May 1899; McKinstry to Markham, 12 June; to Johnston, 13 June; to Cook, 24 June; to Sperry, 6, 12 July; to Wilson, 6 July 1899, RG

77, Entry 1164, Box 1a; Sperry to McKinstry, 20 July; Johnston to McKinstry, 21 June; Markham to McKinstry, 15 June 1899, RG 77 Entry 1170, Box 1, EP; McKinstry to Sperry, 28 September; to Commanding Officer, Augusta Arsenal, 28 September; to Capt. C. A. F. Flagler, Montgomery, AL, 28 September 1899, RG 77, Entry 1164, Box 1a, EP; U.S. Army, Corps of Engineers, *Annual Report*, 1899, 1: 889.

Chapter 13: Topographical Changes

1. *U.S. Field Notes*, 238: 631–32; Gold, *History*, 118.
2. *U.S. Field Notes*, 238: 613; Antonio Alvarez trans. of Samuel Eastlake's 1792 Spanish Survey, 2 August 1838, RG 26.
3. *U.S. Field Notes*, 238: 619.
4. Ibid., 620–22.
5. E. S. Barrouez, Robert Brigelow, and J. W. Lester, 16 January 1833, RG 217; Article of Agreement, 28 August 1834, RG 217; N.d. map by J. Coffee, RG 217.
6. Able S. Baldwin to Gen. J. G. Totten, 3 November 1853, RG 77.
7. Craig, "Mayport Lights," 165.
8. "History of the St. Johns River Lighthouses, 1830–1929."
9. Scull, "Interviews."
10. Florida Inland Navigation District, *The Florida Intercoastal Waterway*, n.p.
11. H. Doc. 586/69/2, 10.
12. Florida Inland Navigation District, *Florida Intercoastal Waterway*, n.p.
13. U.S. Army, Corps of Engineers, *Annual Report*, 1930, 1: 769–70.
14. H. Doc. 180/75/1, 13.
15. U.S. Navy, "Chronological History," 5.
16. U.S. Navy, Naval History Division, *Dictionary of American Naval Fighting Ships*, 3: 172; *Mayport Sextant*, 29 March 1946.
17. "Carrier Based at Mayport in Service," *Seafarer*, November 1952, 1.
18. H. Doc. 519/89/2, 35.
19. H. Doc. 273/89/1, 30; *Florida Times-Union*, 27 July 1938.
20. U.S. Army, Corps of Engineers, *Annual Report*, 1982, 9: 21.

Chapter 14: Fire and Wars

1. "Tall Stacks and Paddlewheels," *Jacksonville Seafarer*, May 1952, 10.
2. Ward, *Old Hickory's Town*, 175–86.
3. "Tall Stacks," 10.
4. James Robertson Ward, "Steamships on St. Johns," *Florida Times-Union*, 2 July 1987.
5. James Robertson Ward, "The Morning After the Fire," *Florida Times-Union*, 2 July 1987.
6. "Tall Stacks," 10.
7. Ibid.
8. Ibid.
9. Ward, "Steamships on St. Johns."
10. "Tall Stacks," 11.
11. Ibid.
12. *Florida Times-Union*, 4, 8 June 1918.

13. Ibid., 4 June 1918; Ward, *Old Hickory's Town*, 199–200.

14. "Tall Stacks," 11–12.

15. S. Doc. 307/71/3, 2: 157–59; 4: 105–06.

16. *Florida Times-Union*, 4 June 1920.

17. Ibid., 31 October 1921.

18. Ibid., 9, 14 November 1923; 18 January 1924; *Laws of Florida*, Special Acts, 2: 3539.

19. *Florida Times-Union*, 6 February 1924.

20. Ibid., 17 June 1924; James A. Carter, "Florida and Rumrunning," 51.

21. Carter, "Florida and Rumrunning," 52–53.

22. "Tall Stacks," 12.

23. Carter, "Florida and Rumrunning," 53.

24. *Florida Times-Union*, 20 January 1928.

25. Ibid., 10 January 1929.

26. Blandford, "Clyde Line," 6–9.

27. *Florida Times-Union*, 17 December 1931.

28. "ILA," 14–15.

29. Bulkley, *At Close Quarters*, 52–58.

30. "Tall Stacks," 12.

31. *Florida Times-Union*, 18, 19 February 1943.

32. Interview with Joe Pickett, librarian at Mayport Naval Station, and viewing U.S. Navy photographs of the Russian crews at Mayport.

33. *Florida Times-Union*, 16 June 1945.

34. Blandford, "Clyde Line," 7–9.

35. *Florida Times-Union*, 22 January 1946.

Chapter 15: The Container Revolution and the JPA

1. Coverdale & Colpitts, "Port," 20–35.

2. Rath, "Florida—The Ferryland," 4–5.

3. "TMT Seatruck Lloyd Launched May 22," *Seafarer*, June 1956, 4–5.

4. *1986 Jacksonville Port Handbook*, 24.

5. Morse, "Rolling Containers," 12.

6. Jelovchan, "Jacksonville," 5.

7. Connor, "From Rags to Riches," 15–16.

8. *Florida Times-Union*, 1 October 1963.

9. *Seafarer*, October 1963, 3.

10. Connor, "From Rags to Riches," 17–18.

11. *Florida Times-Union*, 1 April 1984; *Seafarer*, September 1973, 14.

12. *Florida Journal of Commerce*, June 1972, 6–7.

13. *Seafarer*, September 1973, 14; ibid., March 1974, 12; ibid., September 1974, 14–15.

14. Ibid., September 1974, 14–15; ibid., March 1976, 2–5.

15. *Florida Trend*, January 1975, 96; *Florida Times-Union*, 1 April 1984.

16. *Florida Times-Union*, 17 July 1981, 1 January 1983, 1 April 1984.

17. Hagy, "Port," 46.

18. Ibid., 46–47.

19. O'Riley, "Jaxport's Intermodal Connections," 20–21.

20. Jelovchan, "COSMOS," 3–4.
21. Hagy, "Port," 48.
22. Ibid., 49.
23. *Florida Times-Union*, 8 November 1989.
24. Miller, "JPA's Ship," "Nonunion," Hagy, "Port," 46.
25. "ILA," 15–16; Miller, "Longshoreman."
26. *Florida Times-Union*, 9 November 1989.
27. Ibid., 28 August 1990.
28. Ibid., 28 June 1989.
29. Ibid., 13 October 1989.
30. Ibid.
31. Ibid., 3 June 1990.
32. Ibid.
33. Ibid., 30, 31 October, 1990.
34. Miller, "On the Waterfront"; *1986 Jacksonville Port Handbook*, passim.
35. *1986 Jacksonville Port Handbook*, 40–41.

Bibliography

Alger, Russell A. *The Spanish-American War.* New York: Harper and Brothers, 1901.

Alvarez, Antonio, Translation of Samuel Eastlake's 1792 Spanish Survey, 2 August 1838. USCG Lighthouse Sites, St. Johns River (FL. No. 38), RG 26.

American State Papers: Military Affairs. 7 vols. Washington DC: GPO, 1832–1860.

Ammen, Daniel. *The Old Navy and the New.* Philadelphia: J. B. Lippincott, 1891.

Anderson, Edward Clifford. *Florida Territory in 1844: The Diary of Master Edward Clifford Anderson, USN.* Edited by W. Stanley Hoole. University, AL: University of Alabama Press, 1977.

Arana, Luis R. "A Bicentennial Calendar of British East Florida." *El Escribano* 13 (April 1976): 25–50; (July 1976): 63–101.

Army and Navy Chronicle. Washington, DC. 1835–1842.

Baldwin, Able S. "St. Johns Bar." *The Semi-Tropical* 2: (1876) 321–40.

Bache, A. D. *Report on the Harbor of Charleston, S.C.* Charleston: Steam Power Press of Walker, Evans & C., 1858.

Benjamin, S. G. W. "The Sea Islands." *Harpers New Monthly Magazine* 57: 839–61.

Bennett, Charles E. *Southernmost Battlefields of the Revolution.* Bailey's Cross Roads, VA: Blair, 1970.

——— . *Three Voyages by René Laudonnière.* Gainesville: The University Presses of Florida, 1975.

Benton, Elbert J. *International Law and Diplomacy of the Spanish-American War.* Gloucester, MA: Peter Smith, 1968.

Black, William L. *Hopper Dredging and the Army Engineers.* Atlanta: GPO, 1970.

Blakey, Arch Fredric. *Parade of Memories: A History of Clay County, Florida.* Jacksonville: The Drummond Press, 1976.

Blandford, T. R. "Clyde Line—All Visitors Ashore," *Seafarer,* December 1963, 6–9.

Bliss, Tasker H. *Modern Guns and Mortars,* Artillery Circular 1, Series of 1899. Washington, DC: GPO, 1895.

Brown, Charles H. *The Correspondents' War: Journalists in the Spanish-American War.* New York: Charles Scribner's Sons, 1967.

Buckman, Henry H. "Letters of Captain Charles Willey." *Papers II.* Jacksonville Historical Society, 1949. 16–22.

Bulkley, Robert J. *At Close Quarters: PT Boats in the United States Navy.* Washington, DC: GPO, 1962.

Butler, Lewis. *The Annals of the King's Royal Rifle Corps.* 5 vols. London: J. Murray, 1913–1932.

Cabell, J. Branch, and Alfred J. Hanna. *The St. Johns: A Parade of Diversities.* New York: Farrar & Rinehart, 1943.

"Carrier Based at Mayport in Service," *Seafarer,* November 1952, 1.

Carter, Clarence E., ed. *Territorial Papers of the United States: Florida Territory.* vols. 22–25. Washington, DC: GPO, 1956–1962.

Carter, James A., III. "Florida and Rumrunning During National Prohibition." *Florida Historical Quarterly* 48: 47–56.

Clark, William Bell., ed. *Naval Documents of the American Revolution.* 9 vols. Washington, DC: GPO, 1964–.

Connor, Ann. "From Rags to Riches: The JPA Celebrates Its 25th Anniversary." *JAXPORT,* Winter 1989, 13–19.

Coverdale & Colpitts. "Port and Industrial Survey of Jacksonville, Florida, June 20, 1945." New York: Coverdale & Colpitts, 1945.

Craig, James C. "Steamboat Days on the St. Johns River." *Papers III.* The Jacksonville Historical Society, 1954. 138–45.

———. "The Mayport Lights." *Papers III.* The Jacksonville Historical Society, 1954. 164–69.

Crane, Verner, W. *The Southern Frontier, 1670–1732.* 3rd printing. Ann Arbor: The University of Michigan Press, 1964.

Davis, T. Frederick. *History of Jacksonville, Florida and Vicinity, 1513 to 1924.* 1925. Reprint. Gainesville: University of Florida Press, 1964.

Dickison, Mary Elizabeth. *Dickison and His Men: Reminiscences of the War in Florida.* 1890. Reprint. Jacksonville: San Marco Bookstore, 1962.

Dictionary of American Biography. New York: Scribner's, 1943–.

East, Omega G. "St. Augustine During the Civil War." *Florida Historical Quarterly* 31: 75–91.

Fineren, W. W. "Conditions Adverse to Harbor Construction on the Florida East Coast." In *Florida Engineering Society Year Book*, 1920.

———. "Historical and Financial Summary of the St. Johns River Improvements, 1852–1936." Typescript in U.S. Corps of Engineers, Jacksonville District, Library, n.d.

Fleetwood, Rusty. *Tidecraft: The Boats of Lower South Carolina & Georgia*. Savannah: Coastal Heritage Society, 1982.

Florida Inland Navigation District. *The Florida Intercoastal Waterway from the St. Johns River to Miami, Florida*. Jacksonville: M. & W. B. Drew Co. [1935?].

Florida State Archives, Tallahassee, Florida. Record Groups 101 and 197.

Francke, Arthur E. Jr. *Fort Mellon, 1837–42: A Microcosm of the Second Seminole War*. Miami: Banyan Books, Inc. 1977.

Godoy, Gustavo J. "José Alejandro Huau: A Cuban Patriot in Jacksonville Politics." *Florida Historical Quarterly* 54: 196–206.

Gold, Pleasant Daniel. *History of Duval County Including Early History of East Florida*. St. Augustine: The Record Company, 1929.

Great Britain Public Records Office, Colonial Office, 5/555.

Hagy, James R. "Port of Jacksonville Counts Its Blessings," *Florida Trend*, October 1988, 46–49.

Hamersly, L. R. *A Naval Encyclopaedia*. Philadelphia: L. R. Hamersly & Co., 1881.

Hanna, Alfred Jackson, and Kathryn Abbey Hanna. *Florida's Golden Sands*. New York: The Bobbs-Merrill Company, Inc., 1950.

Hayes, J. D., ed. *S. F. Du Pont Civil War Letters*. Ithaca, N.Y.: Cornell University Press, 1969.

"History of the St. Johns River Lighthouses, 1830–1929." Brochure. Beaches Area Historical Society, Inc. n.d.

"ILA, 1936–1986, Golden Anniversary." Jacksonville: International Longshoremen's Association, Local 1408. 1986.

Jelovchan, Marc. "COSMOS Brings Jacksonville On-line With The World's Cargo." *JAXPORT*, Spring 1989, 3–6.

———. "Jacksonville: The Nation's Ultimate Carport For More Than 25 Years," *JAXPORT*, Summer 1989, 3–6.

Johns, John E. *Florida During the Civil War*. Gainesville: University of Florida Press, 1963.

Laws of Florida.

Lyon, Eugene. "Forts Caroline and San Mateo: Vulnerable Outposts." Typescript in Fort Caroline National Memorial Library, Jacksonville, FL, 1982.

Martin, Richard A., transcriber. "Minute Book: Jacksonville Board of Trade, June 26, 1867–May 21, 1871." Jacksonville Historical Society Archives.

———. *The City Makers*. Jacksonville: Convention Press, Inc., 1972.

Martin, Richard A; and Daniel L. Schafer. *Jacksonville's Ordeal by Fire: A Civil War History*. Jacksonville: Florida Publishing Company, 1984.

Matloff, Maurice. *American Military History*. Washington, DC: GPO, 1965.

May, Philip S. "Zephaniah Kinglsey, Nonconformist (1765–1843)." *Florida Historical Quarterly* 23: 145–159.

Mayport Sextant. U.S. Naval Station Mayport paper.

Miller, Mark R. "JPA's Ship Sails in as Business Booms." *Florida Times-Union*, 11 January 1988.

———. "Longshoreman Remembers Low Wages, Long Workdays." *Florida Times-Union*, 25 October 1987.

———. "Nonunion Labor Making Presence Felt at JPA." *Florida Times-Union*, 24 May 1987.

———. "On The Waterfront." *Florida Times-Union*, 25 October 1987.

Morse, Clarence G. "Rolling Containers—What Is The Outlook." *Seafarer*, November 1956, 12.

Mowat, Charles L. *East Florida as a British Province, 1763–1784*. 1943. Reprint. Gainesville: University of Florida Press, 1964.

Mueller, Edward A. *St. Johns River Steamboats*. Jacksonville: Privately printed, 1986.

———. "Steamboat Activity in Florida During the Second Seminole Indian War." *Florida Historical Quarterly* 64: 407–431.

Niles' Weekly Register. Baltimore, 1811–1849.

1986 Jacksonville Port Handbook. Jacksonville: Seafarer, 1985.

O'Brien, John. *A Captain Unafraid*. New York: Harper and Bros., 1912.

Official Records of the Union and Confederate Navies in the War of the Rebellion. 31 vols. Washington, DC: GPO, 1894–1922.

O'Riley, Tim. "Jaxport's Intermodal Connections." *JAXPORT*, Winter 1989, 20–23.

Paine, Ralph D. *Roads of Adventure*. New York: Houghton Mifflin Company, 1922.

Parker, Susan R. "Canoes: Workaday Watercraft in Eighteenth-Century East Florida." *El Escribano* 24: 56–62.

Parry, J. H., and P. M. Sherlock. *A Short History of the West Indies*. 2nd ed. London: Macmillan & Co. Ltd., 1963.

Patrick, Rembert W. *Florida Fiasco: Rampant Rebels on the Georgia-Florida Border, 1810–1815*. Athens: University of Georgia Press, 1954.

Pennington, Edgar L. "East Florida in the American Revolution, 1775–1778." *Florida Historical Quarterly* 9: 24–46.

Potter, E. B., and Chester W. Nimitz, eds. *Sea Power: A Naval History.* Englewood Cliffs: Prentice-Hall, 1960.

Proctor, Samuel. *Napoleon Bonaparte Broward: Florida's Fighting Democrat.* Gainesville: University of Florida Press, 1950.

Rahn, Ruby A. *River Highway for Trade: The Savannah.* Savannah: GPO, 1968.

Rath, Eric. "Florida—The Ferryland." *Seafarer,* February 1956, 4–5.

Rawls, Oscar G. "Ninety-six Years of Engineering Development on the St. Johns River." *Papers II* Jacksonville Historical Society, 1949. 45–61.

Reiger, John F. "Florida After Secession: Abandonment By The Confederacy and Its Consequences." *Florida Historical Quarterly* 50: 128–42.

Rickenbach, Richard V. "Filibustering with the Dauntless." *Florida Historical Quarterly* 28: 231–53.

Robinson, Calvin L. "An Account of Some of My Experiences in Florida During the Rise and Progress of the Late Rebellion." Typescript in Jacksonville Historical Society's Archives.

Scull, Eleanor. "Interviews of Local Jacksonville Residents (1963–1941); Memoirs and Personal Reminiscences." Corse File. Jacksonville Public Library.

Siebert, Wilbur H. *Loyalists in East Florida, 1774–1785.* Deland, FL: Florida State Historical Society, 1929.

[Simmons, William Hayne.] *Notices of East Florida, With An Account of the Seminole Nation of Indians.* 1822. Reprint. Gainesville: University of Florida Press, 1973.

Smiley, Nixon. *Florida: Land of Images.* Miami: E. A. Seemann Publishing, Inc., 1972.

Smith, W. Calvin. "Mermaids Riding Alligators." *Florida Historical Quarterly,* 54: 443–64.

Snodgrass, Dena. "A River of Many Names." *Papers V.* Jacksonville Historical Society, 1969. 1–4.

Sprague, John T. *The Origin, Progress, and Conclusion of the Florida War.* 1848. Reprint. Gainesville: University of Florida Press, 1964.

Taggart, Robert. *Evolution of the Vessels Engaged in the Waterborne Commerce of the United States.* Washington, DC: U.S. Army Engineer Water Resources Support Center, 1983.

"Tall Stacks and Paddlewheels." *Jacksonville Seafarer,* May 1952.

Tebeau, Charlton W. *A History of Florida.* 7th ed. Coral Gables: University of Miami Press, 1980.

TePaske, John J. *The Governorship of Spanish Florida, 1700–1763.* Durham: Duke University Press, 1964.

"TMT Seatruck Lloyd Launched May 22." *Seafarer,* June 1956.

Trenholm, George A. *Report of the Commissioners for the Improvement of the Port of Charleston.* Charleston: Walker, Evans & Co., 1858.

U.S. Army, Corps of Engineers. *Annual Report of the Chief of Engineers.* Washington, DC: GPO.

———. *United States Coast Defense, 1775–1950: A Bibliography,* Dale E. Floyd, comp. Washington, DC: GPO, 1985.

———, Jacksonville District. "Duval County Beaches Florida, General Design Memorandum, August, 1975." Jacksonville: GPO, 1975.

———, Water Resources Support Center. *The Ports of Jacksonville and Fernandina Beach Florida.* Washington, DC: GPO, 1986.

U.S. Congress Serial Set [Doc. no./congressional no./session no.]:

Ex. Doc. 1/14/1.

Ex. Doc. 49/49/1.

H. Doc. 3/25/2.

H. Doc. 37/85/1.

H. Doc. 61/23/1.

H. Doc. 104/21/2.

H. Doc. 109/79/1.

H. Doc. 180/75/1.

H. Doc. 194/75/1.

H. Doc. 273/89/1.

H. Doc. 519/89/2.

H. Doc. 586/69/2.

S. Doc. 36/54/2.

S. Doc. 307/71/3.

U.S. *Field Notes.* Florida Department of Natural Resources, Division of State Lands, Bureau of State Land Management.

U.S. National Archives:

RG 24. "Records of the Bureau of Naval Personnel."

RG 26. "Records of the United States Coast Guard, USCG Lighthouse Sites, St. Johns River (Fl. No. 38)."

RG 45. "Letters Received by the Secretary of the Navy From Officers Below The Rank of Commander ('Officers Letters'), 1802–1884."

RG 77. "Records of the Office of the Chief of Engineers."

RG 217. "Records of the United States General Accounting Office, Contracts, Ala-Fla, 1799–1864."

U.S. Navy. "Chronological History of the U.S. Naval Auxiliary Air Station Mayport, Florida: History of the Site Since Its Purchase by the Navy." Typescript. Public Relations office, Mayport Naval Air Facility.

U.S. Navy, Naval History Division. *Civil War Naval Chronology, 1861–1865.* Washington, D.C.: GPO, 1971.

———, *Dictionary of American Naval Fighting Ships.* Vol. 3 of 8. Washington, D.C.: GPO, 1968.

Ward, James Robertson. *Old Hickory's Town: An Illustrated History of Jacksonville.* Jacksonville: Florida Publishing Company, 1982.

——— . "Steamships on St. Johns." *Florida Times-Union*, 2 July 1987.

——— . "The Morning After the Fire." *Florida Times-Union*, 2 July 1987.

The War of the Rebellion: A Compilation of the Official Records of the Union and Confederate Armies. 128 vols. Washington, D.C.: GPO, 1880–1901.

Waterbury, Jean Parker. ed. *The Oldest City: St. Augustine Saga of Survival.* St. Augustine: St. Augustine Historical Society, 1983.

Williams, John Lee. *The Territory of Florida.* 1837. Reprint. Gainesville: University of Florida Press, 1962.

General Index

See Index of Ship Names for vessels mentioned

A. Bentley & Sons, Inc., 141
Adams, John Q., 33, 39
Adams-Onís Treaty, 31
Alger, Russell A., 118
Alsop, John T., 148
American Revolution, 15–23
American Transport Lines, 162–63
Ammen, Daniel, 60–62, 64
Anderson, Edward Clifford, 45
Anderson, James B., 100
Anderson, Patton, 71
Artego, Colonel, 104
Atlantic Dry Dock, 166
Atlantic Marine, Inc., 166

Bailey, C. R., 151
Baker, John, 19
Baldwin, Abel Seymour, 46–50, 88–89, 91, 98, 130
Balsam, Henry, 54, 64
Barnwell, John, 11
Barrs, John, M., 99
Baya, H. T., 82
Baya Line, 79
Beerbower, Captain, 85
Bellinger Division (part of JSI), 163

Benyaurd, William H. H., 119–26
Bernard, Simon, 33
Bisbee, Cyrus, 52, 100
Black, William M., 94
Blount Island, 98, 158–59, 161–62, 164–66
Bloxham, William D., 118
Bonham, Thomas S., 124–25
Bowles, William Augustus, 25
Brannan, John Milton, 65
Bravo, Christobal, 59
Brock, Jacob, 46, 52, 55, 73, 75, 76
Brock Line (1852), 46, 52, 55, 73, 77
Broward family, 64
Broward, Mrs. Napoleon B., 106
Broward, Montcalm, 100
Broward, Napoleon B., 99–106, 108
Brown, Charles, 53
Brown, Thomas, 19
Brown Boat Line, 133
Buckley, Frank, 143
Budd, Thomas A., 59–60

Campbell, Charles H., 88–89
Campbell, Hugh, 29
Case, Sam (alias Arthur Foster), 144
Castillo de San Marcos, 6, 10–12
Child, L. Maria, 28
Christopher, John G., 101
Clarke, Elijah, 26
Clinch, Duncan, 43

Clyde Line (1886), 78, 85, 109, 118, 136, 138–40, 147, 151, 157
Coligny, Gaspard de, 3
Collazo, Emilio, 100–101
Collins, C. Curtis, 145
Cook, John M., 120–21, 125–26
Coolidge, Calvin, 145
Cooper, Charles M., 84, 119–20
Corps of Engineers. See U.S. Army, Corps of Engineers
Cow Ford, 15, 17–19, 21, 26, 27, 39
Coxetter, Louis M., 51–52, 75
Crane, L. C., 64–65
Crane, Stephen, 100, 112–14
Crawford, Captain, 83
Crill, E. S., 84–85
Crowley Maritime Corp., 162, 165
Cullum, George W., 89
Cummer, W. W., 119–20
Curry, Captain, 40

Dames Point, 95, 165
Dancy, F. L., 63
Daniel, Robert, 11
Daniels, James T., 148
Daubeney, George, 92
Davis, Jefferson, 51–52, 62
Davis, R. W., 120, 122
Davis, Vernon A., 134
Dawley, T. R., Jr., 112
DeBary Line (1876), 77
De Bry, Theodore, 3
De Cottes, George A., 99–100
De Gorgues, Dominique, 5
DeMariano, Paul D., 160–65
D'Estaing, Count, 25
Dewees, Andrew, 128–29
Dickison, J. J., 71–72
Dillon, Benjamin F., 121–23, 125
Dimmling, Arno, 162
Dowling, W. A., 144–45
Drake, Francis, 6
Dravo Basic Materials, Inc., 162
Drayton, Percival, 66
Dunham, Joseph L., 65
DuPont, Samuel F., 54–56, 59–61, 65, 68
Durkee, J. H., 92, 120, 124
Duval, H. S., 128–29

Eads, James B., 91
Eastern Seaboard Petroleum Company, 166

Edwards, Drover, 71
Einig, John, 120
Elbert, Samuel, 19
Elphinstone, Keith, 22
Estrozi, Nicolas, 6

Ferris, Darius, 128–29
Finegan, Joseph, 64–65
Fisk, Walter L., 92–93
Florida Coastline & Transportation Company, 131–32
Florida East Coast Railroad, 84, 109, 132
Florida Steamship Company (1883), 78
Florida Yacht Club, 108
Floyd, A. B., 129
Floyd, James, 107–8
Floyd, Joseph F., 129
Floyd, Richard G., 63
Fort Caroline, 3–4, 95
Fort San Mateo, 2, 4–5
Fort San Nicolás, 26
Foster, Arthur. See Sam Case
Frazier, Laurence V., 132
Fritot, Alfonso W., 100–101, 106–7, 109–10, 116
Fuller, W. F., 84
Fulton Cutoff, 97–98

Gadsden, James, 33–36
Ganzel, Neal, Jr., 161
Gate Maritime Properties, Inc., 164
George D. Auchter Company, 150
Gibbs Gas Engine of Florida Shipyard, 150
Gillmore, Quincy Adams, 88–90, 92–94
Godolphin, Sidney, 8
Gómez, Máximo, 109, 111, 114
Govin, Charles, 105
Graham, Colin, 18
Grant, James (Baltimore mechanic), 36
Grant, James (governor), 15–16
Grant, William, 17–18
Gray, John C., Jr., 72
Green Cove Maritime, Inc., 163
Guerra, Benjamin, 100
Guerra, Francisco, 9
Gulliver, Louis J., 148

Hagy, James R., 160
Hall, Durham, 61
Hallowes, Colonel, 44
Hand, Somers, 91
Harris, S. W., 36

Hart, Ambrose, 74
Harts, W. W., 123–25
Harvesta Chemical Compounding Company, 86
Hawkins, John, 3
Hearst, William Randolph, 109, 111–12
Hemming, J. C., 57–58
Herbert, Lieutenant, 44
Hester, William, 22
Hogart (Western Union laborer), 124–25
Holmes, Sam P., 139
Hopkins, Charles F., 65
Houston, Edward, 124–25
Howard, Carlos, 25–27
Huau, José Alejandro, 99–101, 106, 109–10, 114, 116
Huckins Yacht Corp., 149–50
Huston, George, 60–61

International Longshoreman's Association, Local #1408, 148, 162–63
Intracoastal Waterway, 33–38, 131–33
Israel (slave), 65

Jackson, Andrew, 31, 34, 39
Jacksonville: Civil War, 51–72; founding, 39; port development, 32–38, 88–98, 133–34, 153–58, 160–62, 164–65; Second Seminole War, 39–50; Spanish-American War, 117–27; Steamboat era, 73–87
Jacksonville Beach, 103, 144–46
Jacksonville Board of Trade, 88, 91, 95, 98
Jacksonville Bulk Terminals, 166
Jacksonville Electric Authority, 159
Jacksonville Port Authority, 98, 153, 157–58, 160–65
Jacksonville Shipyard, Inc., 157, 163–65
Jai, Anna Madgigene, 28
Jefferson, Thomas, 25, 32
Jesup, Thomas S., 37, 44–45
J. M. Murdock Company, 141
Johnston, R. P., 125
Jollie, Martin, 17
Jordon, Thomas, 20–21
JSI. See Jacksonville Shipyard, Inc.

Kilgore, W. F., 103, 109
Kindelan, Sebastián, 29–30
King's Road, 15, 16, 19
Kingsley, Zephaniah, Sr., 27
Kingsley, Zephaniah, Jr., 27–30, 34
Kirwin, Martin E., 157

Lafayette, Marquis de, 25
Lara, Ross, and Company, 92
Laudonnière, René Goulaine de, 3–4
Lee, Robert E., 55, 75
Le Moyne, Jacques, 3–4
Lewis, William, 108–9
Leyte Vidal, Francisco, 104
Lowry, Sumter L., 148
Lucas, J. E., 85
Ludlow, William, 88–89

McCready, Ernest W., 100, 110–11, 114
MacDuff, William A., 121
McGiffin, John, 156
McGiffin & Co., Inc., 156
McGirt, Daniel, 24–25
McIntosh, George, 27
McIntosh, John, 27
McIntosh, John Houstoun, 27–30
McIntosh, Lachlan, 18
Mackay, Hugh, 12
McKee, J. A., 96
McKeige, Edward, 67
McKinstry, Charles H., 126–27
Mackroth, John, 160
McNelty, William T., 46
McQueen, John (Don Juan), 25–27, 129
Madison, James, 28
Mallory Line, 78
Mansfield, Joseph K. F., 36–38, 44–45
Marqués, Juan Menéndez, 9
Martí, José, 100
Martin, John, 17
Mather, S. W., 60
Mathews, George, 26, 28–29
Mathews, John, 156
Mayport, 45, 103, 108, 129–31, 144–45
Mayport Naval Station. See U.S. Mayport Naval Station
Mayport Naval Station Division (part of JSI), 163
Mellon, W. L., 140
Melton, Ona, 102
Mendoza, C. Cliff, 164–65
Menéndez de Avilés, Pedro, 1–2, 4–6
Menéndez Marqués, Pedro, 6
Merchants and Miners Line, 96
Meriam, Frank B., 69
Merrill, Alexander, 103, 118–19, 122, 136, 138, 140
Merrill, James C., 151

Merrill, J. Eugene, 126, 136, 138, 140
Merrill, Kenneth Alexander, 140
Merrill-Stevens Shipyard, 86, 97, 103, 126, 136–43, 146, 150–52
Milton, John, 62
Monroe, Jack P., 134
Monroe, James, 31
Moore, James, 11
Moran, William, 71
Moran Towing and Transportation Company, 155
Morey & Thomas, 141
Mowbray, John, 18–21
Mud machine, 30–38
Murphy, Edward, 113
Myers, C. H., 145
Myers family, 62

Nicholson, J. W. A., 59, 62, 64
Nombre de Dios, 12–13
North Florida Shipyards, 165
Núñez, Emilio, 100, 104, 106, 108–9, 112

O'Brien, John, 100, 106–11, 114–16
Ocean Steamship Company, 78
Offshore Power Systems (OPS), 158–59, 164
Oglethorpe, James, 12–13
Operation Desert Shield, 165
OPS. See Offshore Power Systems
O'Rourke, John J., 124–25

Pablo Beach See Jacksonville Beach.
Paine, Ralph D., 100, 109–12, 114
Palmer, David L., 128–29
Palmer, John, 12–13
Patriots War, 29
Peace, Robert C., 158
Pearson, J. W., 63
Peck, Fenn, 44
Perry, Charles, 146
Piercy, William P., 41–42
Plant Investment Company, 77
Post, James C., 93
Post, John, 80–82
Prevost, Augustine, 18
Prohibition, 142–47

Quesada, Gonzalo de, 100
Quesada, Juan Nepomuceno de, 25–27

Rath, Eric, 154–55
Rawls, Dave, 157

Rawls Brothers Shipyard, 157
Ray's Steam Schooner Line, 78
Reddig, George, 148
Revenel and Company (1865), 74–75
Ribault, Jacques, 4
Ribault, Jean, 1–5
Roads, Calvin, 41
Rodgers, C. R. P., 55, 59
Rolle, Denys, 16
Ross, Roderick G., 92–93, 119
Rossell, William T., 94
Rubens, Horatio S., 106–7

St. Augustine, 51, 54, 57, 62, 132, 147; attacked by the English, 11–13; construction of Castillo de San Marcos, 10; as an English colony, 15–23; Drake attacks, 6; founded, 4, 6–7; occupied during the Civil War, 59, 69, 71–72; Picolata becomes river port for, 9, 42; port of entry, 5; Second Spanish period, 24–31; struggle with the French, 1–6
St. Johns Bluff, 21–22, 39, 42, 64–65, 95, 120–27
St. Johns Division, 157
St. Johns River: Corps of Engineers develops, 33–38, 88–98; defense of, 117–27; dugout restricts the use of, 8–9, 24; early commercial trade, 22–23, 39–41, 42, 46, 73–83, 154–56; as a military highway, 10–12, 24, 26–27, 29–30, 43–45; naming of, 1–2; used as a moat, 1, 6–7, 15–16, 18–19, 21–22, 24; water hyacinths in, 83–87
St. Johns River Shipbuilding Company, 141
St. Johns Town, 22–23
Sanborn, Frank, 71
Saturiba, Chief, 2, 5
Savannah Line (1845), 46
Scott, James, Jr., 158
Scott, Winfield, 37, 44
Scovell, Sylvester, 100
Scull, W. E., 131
Sea-Land Service, Inc., 155–57, 162
Shaw, W. A., 84
Shorstein, Harry, 159
Shreve, Henry M., 78
Simmons, Richard, 165

Simmons, William, 32
Smith, C. B., 121
Smith, Thomas Adam, 29–30
Spencer, Charles F., 163
Sperry, Charles, 127
Standard American Company, 96
Steedman, Charles, 53–54, 65, 68
Stephens, Winston, 58, 64
Stevens, Arthur, 136, 140
Stevens, Thomas H., 58, 68
Stowe, Calvin E., 76
Stowe, Harriet Beecher, 76
Strachan Shipping Co., 156

Tanzler, Hans, 158
Tatnall, Isaac, 54
Taylor, Cornelius, 128–30
Thomas, (slave), 25
Thompson, Samuel B., 74
TMT Trailer Ferry, Inc., 154–56, 165–66
Tombs family, 62
Tonyn, Patrick, 16–18, 20–24
Totten, Joseph G., 49
Traiper, James H., 55
Trenchard, Stephen, 50

U.S. Army, Corps of Engineers: and beach renourishment, 135; and defense of the St. Johns River, 119–27; developing the St. Johns River, 49–50, 88–98, 130–31, 157; and Intracoastal Waterway, 33–38, 132; and Second Seminole War, 44–45; and water hyacinths, 84–87
U.S. Gypsum Company, 166
U.S. Mayport Naval Station, 98, 133–34, 150–51, 166
U.S. Navy Fuel Depot, 166

Vogel, Leo, 81–82

Ware, Roger, 145
Washington, George, 25
Water hyacinths, 83–87
Webber, H. J., 85
Welles, Gideon, 56
Willey, Charles, 40–41, 54, 59
Williamson, Thomas, 22
Wilson, John M., 119–20, 122
Woodhull, Maxwell, 62, 67–68
Wright, Horatio C., 49–50, 130

Youngberg, Gilbert A., 132

Zespedes, Vicente Manuel de, 24

INDEX OF SHIP NAMES

The year indicates the period covered in the text

Agnus Manning (1906), schooner, 139
Alert (1861), schooner, 54
Alexander Jones (1897), 114
Algonquin (1925), cruise ship, 147, 151
Algonquin (1880s), steamer, 78
America (1861), yacht, 52, 53, 57, 58, 68
Arapahoe (1918), steamer, 141
Argo (1831), schooner, 42
Arrow (1861), schooner, 53
Atlantic (1916), dredge, 96, 141

Benjamin Franklin (1943) Liberty Ship, 150
Bienville (1860), US steamer, 53
Biscayne (1897), steamer, 114
Biscayne (1912), tug, 96
Boutwell (1896), US revenue cutter, 101, 103, 108, 109, 113

Camden (1837), steamer, 45
Cameron (1903), barge, 139
Camilla (1861), yacht, 52
Carib Queen (1956), 155
Carolina (1670), 9
Cecile (1861), steamer, 51, 52
Chatham (1912), steamship, 96
Cherokee (1925), cruise ship, 147, 151

Cherokee (1886), steamer, 78
City of Birmingham (1880s), steamer, 78
City of Fayetteville (1903), steamer, 139
City of Jacksonville (1880s), steamer, 79, 84
City of Key West (1896), steamer, 105
City of Palatka (1878), steamer, 78
City Point (1865), steamer, 74, 75
Columbine (1864), tug, 71
Comanche (1880s), steamer, 78
Commodore (1896), tug, 104, 106–10, 112–14, 116
Competitor (1896), schooner, 102, 104
Congree (1929), US pipeline dredge, 132
Constitution (1931), US frigate, 147, 148

D-1 (1929), US snagboat, 132
Dale (1861), US sloop-of-war, 53
Darien (1833), steamer, 40
Darlington (1849), steamer, 46, 52, 55, 58, 66, 73, 75
Dauntless (1896), tug, 100, 106–9, 111–16
Davenport (1836), steamer, 43
Dictator (1866), steamer, 75, 77, 78
Dreadnought (1778), brig, 21, 22
Duval (1904), ferryboat, 139

E. B. Hale (1862), steamer, 66
Echo. **See** *Jeff Davis*, 51
Edith (1898), tug, 120

Elam (1903), steamer, 139
Eliza Hancox (1880s), steamer, 79
Ellen (1862), steamer, 58
Empire City (1862), schooner, 59. See also Rebecca (schooner)
Essayons (1835), US steamer, 37, 44

Fannie Dugan (1880s), steamer, 79, 80
Fire Island Lightship (1941), 149
Flora (1880s), steamer, 79
Florence (1870s), steamer, 77
Florida (1834), steamer, 42, 43
Florida (1904), US snagboat, 139
Forward (1896), US Coast and Geodetic Survey, 110
Frederick DeBary (1880s), steamer, 79, 139

Galatea (1778), ship, 20
General Hunter (1864), US steamer, 70
General Moultrie (1857), world's first hopper dredge, 89
General Taylor (1844), US steamer, 45
George M. Bird (1880s), steamer, 79
George Washington (1816), steamer, 78
George Washington (1829), steamer, 40
Germaine (1778), 21
Gipsy (1890s), steamer, 86, 87
Governor Milton (1862), steamer, 64–66
Grebe (1931), US minesweeper, 148
Guadalcanal (1944), USS, CVE-60, 134
Gunboat 62 (1812), 29
Gunboat 63 (1812), 29

Harriet Weed (1864), US steamer, 70
Hawke (1777), transport, 18, 19
H. B. Plant (1880s), steamer, 79
Helen Getty (1860s), steamer. See St. Johns (steamer)
Henry Andrew (1862), USS, 60
Henry Burden (1871), hopper dredge, 89–91
Herald (1861), steamer, 52
Hinchenbrook (1776), 17, 20–21
H. T. Baya (1880s), steamer, 79, 80–83

Ida B. (1890s), tug, 85–87
Ideal X (1956), container ship, 156
Impervious (1990), US minesweeper, 165
Iroquois (1880s), steamer, 78
Iroquois (1927), cruise ship, 147. See also Solace
Isaac Smith (1862), US steamer, 59

Jacksonville (1990), barge, 164
Jeff Davis (1861), brig, 51
Jennie Lane (1880s), steamer, 79, 80
Jennie Thomas (1897), schooner, 115
Joeb (1929), derrick boat, 132
John (1870s), brig, 91
John David Mongin (1836), steamer, 43
John Sylvester (1880s), steamer, 79, 80–83
John W. Anderson (1861), steamer. See Mabel
José Padrón (1914), steamer, 140

Kansas City (1880s), steamer, 78
Kate (1861), steamer, 52
Kate Spencer (1896), steamer, 103, 106
Key West (1912), dredge, 96
Kona (1921), yacht, 143, 144

La Gloria (1914), steamer, 140
Larkspur (1918), freighter, 141
Laurada (1896), steamer, 103, 107–8
Le Grande Duchesse (1880s), steamer, 78
Le Reve (1890s), steamer, 86
Lillian (1896), steam launch, 103
Louise F. (1921), auxiliary schooner, 144

Mabel (1861), steamer, 53
McLane (1896), US revenue cutter, 101, 110, 115
Magnolia (1851), steamer, 46
Magnolia (1880s), steamer, 80
Maine (1897), US battleship, 116, 118
Manito II (1924), yacht, 144, 145
Maple Leaf (1864), steamer, 70
Marblehead (1897), US cruiser, 114
Martha Helen (1896), tug, 96, 106, 108, 119
Meredith (1777), 18–19
Mohawk (1925), cruise ship, 147
Mohawk (1918), steamer, 141, 151

Nashville (1890s), US gunboat, 85–86
Neva (1870s), brig, 91
Newark (1896), US cruiser, 110
Nick King (1857), steamer, 75–76. See also St. Mary's
Norwich (1862), US gunboat, 68–69

Ocmulgee (1845), steamer, 46
Orange Maid (1870s), steamer, 76–77
Osceola (1914), steamer, 140, 157
Ottawa (1862), US gunboat, 55–58
Otter (1778), sloop, 22

The Ox (1896), tug, 101. See also *Three Friends*

Palatka (1880), steamer, 80
Pargo (1903), schooner, 139
PC-615 (1943), US patrol craft, 150
Penguin (1862), US gunboat, 59, 60
Perseus (1778), ship, 22
Ponce (1953), motorship, 154
Puerto Rico (1955), 155

Raleigh (1896), US cruiser, 109–10
Ralston (1903), barge, 139
Rebecca (1776), sloop, 18–21
Rebecca (1861), schooner, 54. See also *Empire City*
Red Cloud (1918), composite ship, 141
Ridgewood (1880s), schooner, 91
R. L. Mabey (1896), launch, 108
Rosa (1880s), steamer, 79
Russ (1924), converted sub-chaser, 144–45

San Andrés (1565), shallop, 5
San Augustín del Patrón (1795), galley, 27
St. John (1775), 17–18
St. Johns (1912), dredge, 96
St. Johns (1850s), steamer, 46, 52
St. Johns County (1920), steamer, 143
St. Johns Lightship (1929), USCG, 130
St. Marys (1857), steamer. 46, 52, 54, 57–59, 68–69, 72. See also *Nick King*
St. Matthews (1845), steamer, 46
Santa Mónica (1795), schooner, 26
Santee (1836), steamer, 44–45
Santo Tomás (1795), brig, 26–27
Sarah and Caroline (1861), schooner, 53
Saratoga (1990), USS, CV-60, 165
Seatruck Lloyd (1956), 155
Seminole (1925), cruise ship, 147, 151
Seminole (1850s), steamer, 46
Shawnee (1927), cruise ship, 147, 151
Silver Heels (1897), schooner, 115
Silver Springs (1862), steamer, 64, 77

Simons (1929), pipeline dredge, 132
Skipper Bill (1924), speedboat, 144
Solace (1940), US Hospital Ship, 151. See also *Iroquois*
Solomons (1944), US, CVE-67, 134
Southeast (1918), barge, 141
Spark (1831), US schooner, 41
Specie (1861), schooner, 53
Standbury (1896), schooner, 104
Stephen R. Mallory (1898), schooner, 101
Suwannee (1898), US snagboat, 125

Tarawa (1952), US, CVA-40, 134
Three Friends (1896), tug, 96, 100–101, 103–6, 108–11, 114, 116, 148
Three Kids (1903), steamer, 139
Thunderer (1778), galley, 21–22
Titiritera (1795), gunboat, 27
Trinity (1565), 5
Tuncastle (1776), sloop, 18

Uncas (1862), US gunboat, 64–65, 68

Vagabond (1903), steamer, 139
Vagabondia (1914), houseboat, 140
Vamoose (1897), yacht, 111
Victory (1924), yacht, 146
Volunteer (1912), tug, 96

Wabash (1862), US screw frigate, 58–59
Washington A. Clark (1904), steamer, 139
Welaka (1928), pipeline dredge, 97
Welaka (1851), steamer, 46
Welaka (1880s), steamer, 79
Western Texas (1878), steamer, 78
William Gaston (1845), steamer, 46
William M. Tupper (1914), steamer, 140
Winona (1896), US revenue cutter, 105, 110

Yamacraw (1924), USCG cutter, 145
YMS-348 (1943), US minesweeper, 150
YMS-349 (1943), US minesweeper, 150

Zeeburg (1912), steamship, 96